THE TEACHINGS OF THE GREAT MYSTICS

THE MOST REVEREND KARL PRUTER

BORGO PRESS / WILDSIDE PRESS

www.wildsidepress.com

Table of Contents

MYSTICISM 5

PLOTINUS 15

DIONYSIUS THE AREOPOGITE 20

AUGUSTINE 25

MEISTER ECKHART 32

SUSO, TAULER, AND THE FRIENDS OF GOD 38

THEOLOGIA GERMANICA 45

THE CLOUD OF UNKNOWING 50

NICOLAS HERMAN 55

JACOB BOEHME 60

ST. JOHN OF THE CROSS 64

THE MYSTICAL ELEMENTS IN ENGLISH PURITANISM 68

WILLIAM BLAKE 76

JOHANN G. HAMANN 79

WALT WHITMAN 84

KAHLIL GIBRAN 88

THE AWAKENING 92

PURGATION 98

ILLUMINATION 102

UNION WITH GOD 108

HOW TO BEGIN THE CONTEMPLATIVE LIFE 113

BIBLIOGRAPHY 117

TO CHANNAH
with
love

Chapter I

Mysticism

The Twentieth Century has witnessed a tremendous breakthrough in man's knowledge of the physical universe. The fury of World War II drove man to new discoveries in the field of atomic science, and he quickly utilized his new knowledge to create horrifying weapons of destruction.

I do not know whether there is any significance in the fact that man turned his greatest physical discovery to evil use and is only now painfully and slowly attempting to adapt his new knowledge to peaceful purposes.

The civilization that is capable of such great discoveries could, it would seem to an outsider, be far from savagery. Yet, such is obviously not the case, since we are confronted with the fact that the two most technologically and scientifically advanced nations are seriously contemplating the possibility of utterly destroying each other.

These two advanced nations are not contemplating a mere primitive war where one side, the victor, destroys the other. They are planning and moving toward a war of mutual destruction.

It is obvious to every thinker that the real gap is not the missile gap but the gap between our scientific knowledge of the material world and our scientific knowledge of the spiritual world.

It was apparent at the close of World War II that many of the scientists who worked on the atom bomb suffered a twinge of conscience at this paradox. Man has a modern mind and a stone age soul.

This is not to say that man has not increased his knowledge of spiritual things. Each great period of artistic, material and intellectual activity has brought with it a new wave of men and women who have explored the spiritual universe and reported new findings or new confirmations of old truths.

During the great Classical Period, mystics appeared and charted the spiritual world even as men charted the physical world about them. The same dual activity marked the Medieval and Renaissance periods of history.

During the Fourteenth Century, man, indeed, experienced a spiritual breakthrough. Had he pursued this assiduously, the world would have taken a different course; but the Renaissance brought discoveries in the physical world which diverted man's attention from spiritual things.

The exploration of the physical world is less demanding and, perhaps for this reason, more popular. But, regardless of the reason for it, man, since the Renaissance, has devoted the overwhelming bulk of his energies and resources to the exploration of the material world around him.

Even the Church has joined the ranks of those who deem the physical world as the reality demanding our priority. The Church has increasingly concerned itself with the social, that is the material welfare of its parishioners. Some churches have even argued that you cannot preach to a man with an empty stomach, forgetting that the early Church made its first converts among the hungry, the naked, the enslaved, and the imprisoned.

What I am saying is, we need to devote a greater portion of our energies to the spiritual world in which we live.

First, because it is there, it is a challenge.

Second, while survival for its own sake is vastly overrated, it is better to survive than not to survive.

Third, because the purpose of our creation demands it.

Having decided on a spiritual inquiry, let us seriously consider our starting place. Any scientific inquiry starts with what is already known. The mystics have been the pioneers in the spiritual world, and hence, any study of the spiritual world begins with them.

It is their pioneering spirit that has won for them both praise and condemnation. Eckhart was condemned by the Pope for being a man who "wanted to know too much."

To this, the modern mind is impelled to reply: "Can we ever know too much?" and "Have we not suffered greatly from too little, rather than too much knowledge?"

Certainly, we need to match our material progress by similar spiritual progress. The method of the mystics at first glance seems naively simple, yet it meets every pragmatic test.

The mystic has rejected both the Naturalist's approach to truth and the Platonic Idealist's.

The mystic is equally convinced that the truth of the spirit cannot be found by a study of the physical phenomena about us or the contemplation of philosophical ideas.

Truth, according to the mystic, is unknowable and, at the same time, almost not worth knowing.

Rather than concern ourselves with what we need to know, we should concern ourselves with Whom we need to know. It is not the truth but the Creator of the truth who must be understood, grasped and possessed.

The finite mind of man cannot comprehend the infinite world. Unless man sees with God's eyes and understands with God's mind, he will see only darkly and then only in part.

According to the mystic, we are too concerned with trivialities, or, at best, illusionary manifestations of the one ultimate reality. He pleads with us to find and unite with our Creator. "This," he says, "is man's end; this is God's purpose in man's creation."

It is the spiritual world that beckons, that offers to reveal itself through the Creator. "Seek ye first the Kingdom of God, and all the rest shall be added unto you."

Modern man has turned this around. He vainly hopes to understand his world by learning about it one piece at a time. The mystic is impatient with such piecemeal dissection. "Seek God and know."

It sounds simple, but unfortunately, to the modern mind, fantastic. All too often we have dismissed the findings of the mystics without investigation.

We are like the man who wears a sign: "Please let me do it my way. I do not wish to be confused with the facts." Even a superficial study of the teachings of the great mystics will be sufficient to convince the unbiased inquirer of who it is that has the facts.

The mystic way is easy to understand, less easy to follow and impossible to evaluate incorrectly. In the pages that follow, our brief study of the method, the men and women who have tried it and the scientific study of their findings should enable us to determine whether or not the mystics have the answer to man's search for reality.

What is mysticism? It is an experimental science which seeks to bridge the gulf between man and God. A mystic is one who seeks to unite with God. He takes Christ at His word that we are joint heirs of the Kingdom of God and that we can all be the Sons of God.

The claim does not stop short of making man God and making God man. It is either the great blasphemy of all time or the great hope; but anything which stops short of actual union with God is not classic mysticism.

The mystic seeks no new knowledge about God; he is not searching for a new formula by which he might define God, nor is he seeking new revelations, but rather to unite his soul with God.

Evelyn Underhill defines mysticism as "the expression of the innate tendency of the human spirit towards complete harmony with the transcendental order; whatever by the theological formula under which that order is understood."[1] The end is, of course, the union with God. To unite himself with the Ultimate Reality becomes for the mystic the meaning and purpose of life.

Classical mysticism not only contends that this is possible, but proposes a four-fold path, or spiritual ladder, by which man might pursue this end.

The four-fold path consists of these steps:

First, Conviction or Awakening of Self

Second, Purification

Third, Enlightenment or Illumination

Fourth, Union with God

Let us consider them one by one. The first, Conviction, closely resembles what the evangelicals call "Conversion." However, it is not the acceptance of beliefs or the exchange

---

[1] Evelyn Underhill, "*Mysticism,*" p. XIV.

8

of one set of ideas for another, but rather it is a re-orientation from self-centeredness to God-centeredness.

It is as if the individual, once satisfied to relate every experience and every phenomena to himself, now seeks to relate himself to the One Great Absolute.

Before, Self and Self-survival were the center of the soul's existence and the one great driving force; and suddenly, these cease to matter and are of no concern to the awakened individual.

Thus the self-centered individual now becomes obsessed with a desire to find God and to achieve oneness with Him. He seeks neither to save himself nor to find himself, but literally to lose himself in God.

This awakening, or conviction, may be gradual, coming almost imperceptibly over the years, or it may be a sudden and traumatic experience, as in the case of the Apostle Paul. The awakening is not the end, as many modern fundamentalists seem to think, but the beginning. For Christ, Himself, had this experience at his Baptism and the Master was not sure what it signified until after he spent forty days and forty nights contemplating every aspect of the event.

This withdrawal to intensive contemplation follows almost every mystical awakening. The purpose of the withdrawal varies, but almost always includes a need on the part of the awakened to evaluate the experience.

Some are fearful lest they lose the new sense of direction, others withdraw determined to find with the greatest dispatch, the Deity to whom they now feel drawn with intense longing.

Like Christ, the temptation confronts the mystic to use his new knowledge in profane ways or for selfish ends. All the great mystics abhor the thought that they might treat the experience lightly, and without undertaking the search for God with the thoroughness and diligence which his Greatness merits.

Before their awakening, they felt they were in ignorance of the true nature of the universe or of their own need to relate themselves to God. In ignorance, they were unaccountable for their actions. Not knowing right from wrong, they could not be held responsible. But once having seen, at last, a fleeting glimpse of the Ultimate Reality, and knowing that it is now possible for man to become united with God, any rejection of Him, either by rebellion or simply by neglect, would be so iniquitous, mortal man could not atone for his sin.

Such a thought would drive a man to contemplate long and hard about his future. We are told that Paul spent two years in the desert, but the two years are blank, so we can only imagine the wrestling he did with his soul.

Others, however, have given us accounts, many of which we shall study in the next few chapters. These accounts tell of the new sense of values brought by the awakening of self, and how the individual feels trapped by the knowledge that the awakening has brought to him.

It is, as if, a man were told of a great treasure that awaited him if only he would pursue it with all his strength, with all his mind and all his will. No thought of danger, hardship or any other consideration could deter him from seeking his goal. He must pursue it, even though he knows that once he had not been disturbed by the thought, for its existence to him was unknown; but now that he knows of it, he cannot enjoy his former peace, but must risk all because of what he has learned.

Yet, even as the awakened one is excited and challenged by the glimpse of the road ahead, so is he sickened by the awareness of his own shortcomings. He does not and cannot feel worthy enough to stand in the presence of God; and yet, he now knows that he is being invited to be united with his Creator.

Before this could happen, he must become a worthy vessel for the Divine to inhabit, for the union means not only will he dwell with God, but that God, also, will dwell with him. God does not unite with dross, but with other gold, equally refined and free of dross.

The Purification of Self, the purging of the soul, becomes the stumbling stone in the mystical path. If purgation is possible, it will take many years, and may prove beyond the capacity of the individual to accomplish. Discouragement lies in the way not only because of the sheer labor involved,

10

but more especially since a rational man must constantly be in doubt as to the possibility of achieving it. There are many who will say that it is beyond man's ability to achieve, and many more who will say that man cannot achieve this end without supernatural help.

For, if man could become good, would he be man? If man is by nature evil, how can he change his nature? Much of the mystic's effort is spent in remorse, confession and earnest seeking of God's forgiveness. These are sensitive men who, having perceived the goodness of God, are struck with the full horror of their own transgressions.

To those of us who take our sins more lightly, this concern seems exaggerated, at least when the mystic considers such sins as pride, indifference and attachment to the things of this world.

As we read the Confessions of Jacob Boehme, or even Augustine, we are struck by the fact that their failures, even those we might regard as trifling shortcomings, bring them acute pain and suffering.

Purgation involves something more than just living the Ten Commandments, at least in a narrow sense. It involves the turning away from self and love of self to embrace God and literally lose oneself in Him. "St. Catherine of Genoa, in that crucial hour in which she saw by the light of love her own self-centered and distorted past,cried, 'No more sins!' Yet, she entered into the Purgative Way, and for four years endured repulsive duties in her efforts toward that self-conquest which would make her 'conformable in her own measure' to the dictates of that Pure Love which was the aspect of reality that she had seen?"[2]

The mystic seeks to eradicate self, and by his own contrition, mortification and determination, serve only God and merit God's forgiveness. Irregardless of what the mystic may profess regarding the doctrine of the atonement of Jesus Christ, he finds it necessary to cleanse himself before he feels he merits God's forgiveness. In this respect, no

---

[2] *Ibid.*, p. 201.

mystic can ever be declared by the present creedal denominations to be orthodox.

Only in their insistence that it cannot be done alone, do they once again return to orthodoxy. For example, St. John of Epes, who is the classic authority on the Purgative Way, says:

"In order to overcome our desires and to renounce all those things, our love and inclination for which are wont so to inflame the will that it delights therein, we require a more ardent fire and a nobler love—that of the Bridegroom. Finding her delight and strength in Him, the soul gains the vigour and confidence which enable her easily to abandon all other affections. It was necessary, in her struggle with the attractive force of her sensual desires, not only to have this love for the Bridegroom, but also to be filled with a burning fervour; full of nobler passions we should never cast off the yoke of the senses, nor be able to enter on their night; neither should we have the courage to remain in the darkness of all things, and in denial of every desire."[3]

Purgation involves several clearly defined steps. First, there must be detachment from the sensual things that bind the soul to earth. Second, there must be mortification or the process of finding a positive outlet for a new-found spiritual energy. Whether it is called functioning, or simply a life of Christian action, the soul, having forsaken earthly things, must now become all absorbed in spiritual things. This may consist of constant prayer, or it may include suffering self-inflicted asceticism, which some have carried to extremes. But, for the classic mystic, this period ends when, through Illumination, the mystic is given new direction and new tasks.

Called cosmic consciousness, or simply the sense of the presence of God, the mystic, after he has passed through the purgative state, frequently receives intuitional knowledge which raises his spirits to a high state of ecstasy and makes him the highly productive individual that he is.

---

[3] *Ibid.*, p. 203.

Many of the mystics like Boehme and Blake seemed simple, poorly educated and sometimes, not overly bright; yet they amazed the world by their wisdom and their tremendous productivity. Jacob Boehme, the cobbler of Goelitz, did not go to the intellectuals of Europe, they came and sought him out. In our time, Kahlil Gibran not only produced some outstanding drawings, but also best selling poetry. While it is early to evaluate his poetry, I can assure you that, while it may never have great appeal to the critics, it will continue in its popularity for centuries.

The illumination of the mystics has been examined and explained away in terms of their vitality, or even of self-deception, but their amazing accomplishments are there and cannot be explained away. There were too many mystics, and they accomplished too much for everything to be brought to nought by the glib phrase, the pat explanation or the Freudian rationalizing of the obvious.

Later we shall examine the lives of these men and their accomplishments and form our own conclusions. We may not agree that all of these are divinely inspired, or even that any of them are, but there has to be some explanation for the tremendous outpouring of literary and artistic work of quality. There is something unique in the life of the mystic that makes him unusually creative.

Our evaluation of his claim to Illumination will have a great deal of bearing on our evaluation of his claim to have achieved, even for a fleeting moment, a union with God. The idea that an individual can achieve an utter transmutation of the self in God is so fantastic, at first thought, that we instinctively reject it.

Yet, Jesus Christ promised us that we would be joint heirs with Him in the Kingdom of God. Since He claimed Sonship with God, if we are to be joint heirs, we cannot be less than sons of God.

St. Anthanasius says, "He became man that we might be made God."[4] Fortunately for the mystics, he said it first, so

---

4 *Ibid.*, p. 419.

that Eckhart might be able to claim to be following the Church Fathers when he wrote, "Our Lord says to every living soul, "I became man for you. If you do not become God for me, you do me wrong."[5]

This claim, and the language in which it is stated, has brought much criticism upon the mystics and has resulted in their being banned and declared heretical on many occasions. But rational, intelligent people cannot reject an idea because it is daring, or because it is stated with the passion of one who has emerged from an ecstatic experience. We have to examine carefully the evidence of the mystical experiences and then draw conclusions. If we examine, fairly, the writings of the mystics and the critical comments of their contemporaries, we shall probably have to conclude they are justified in their claims or, at the very least, conclude that we are incapable of giving judgment. Probably, many of their claims can only be proven or disproven when we are willing to travel the road they traveled. Often we find ourselves in the position of those who listened to the seemingly wild tales of travelers to Cathay or the New World. We are skeptical, but until we, ourselves, have made the journey, we cannot say with certainty that this is or is not true.

I trust that in the pages ahead, we will not only examine the writings of the mystics, and study the accounts of their lives, but become fellow travelers on the road that they have charted for us.

---

[5] *Ibid.*, pp. 419-420.

Chapter II
Plotinus

The mystics have contributed much to art, science, literature, and philosophy, but unfortunately, the world tends to think of them as impractical people. The reason is obvious, for if the mystic produces little of what the world calls "practical," then he is a visionary and a dreamer. If he produces much, the world ceases to think of him as a mystic but rather as an artist or a philosopher who happened to have some mystical tendencies.

Plotinus is an example of a great mystic whom the world regards as a great philosopher and seldom, if ever, thinks of his contribution to mysticism. Yet, the mystical movement owes much to Plotinus, for he, more than anyone else, revealed the religious nature of Greek philosophy. It was Plotinus who prepared the way for the adoption of Greek philosophy by the Christian Church.

Paul and the early Christian thinkers tended to feel that the philosophy of the Greeks was a rival to faith. The Greeks were preoccupied with philosophy, and the intellectuals among them were not attracted to Christianity because they felt it was lacking in thought content.

The Christians, on the other hand, felt that the philosophers were merely concerned with morality, or at best, were so involved in their explanations of life that they failed to respond to the great challenge of life, namely, to come to a decision concerning God. These men were so involved in spinning theories that they were impractical about the challenge of eternal life which had been flung at their world by the coming and the resurrection of Jesus Christ.

Plotinus was favored by circumstance of birth to interpret the best of both schools of thought to his generation. Born in Alexandria about 205 A.D., of Hebrew parents, who had undergone Hellenization, he had an opportunity to study both Hebrew and Greek thought.

Alexandria was the melting pot of the Roman world. Here, in a city ruled by Greeks, Egyptian gods were worshipped in temples that stood beside Greek schools of philosophy. The Jews and the mystery religions of the Near East were represented here, and Roman concepts of law and order held the diverse groups together.

According to his disciple, Porphyry, Plotinus did not show any great passion for philosophy until he was twenty-eight years of age.[1] Then, he became a seeker, going from school to school, and from master to master. He finally found a teacher, Ammonius Saccas, that suited him, and he studied under Saccas for ten years.

He wanted to go to the East and study the ancient religions of the Brahmins and the Magi. The Emperor Gordianus started an expedition to recover Mesopotamia from the Persians, and Plotinus enlisted in his army at the age of thirty-nine.[2]

During the invasion, the Emperor was murdered and mutiny broke out in the army. The eastward drive was brought to a halt. Plotinus stayed for a while in Antioch and then, in 244, when he was forty, he went to Rome where he was to live and work for the remainder of his life.[3]

It was at Rome that Plotinus began to write his philosophical treatises. Here he organized a school and began to teach Platonic philosophy, but heavily larded with mysticism. Like many mystics, Plotinus was not convinced that any good purpose would be served by scattering his writings widely. Consequently, most of his notes and manuscripts were entrusted to his disciple, Porphyry, who was instructed not to divulge his teachings, except to those who might be considered serious initiates.

Rome, in the latter part of the Third Century, was in a constant state of confusion. Enemies from within and without made life precarious, and under these conditions, the philosophy of Plotinus had a special appeal. Like the Christians of the time, Plotinus taught that the world about was

---

[1] Sheldon Cheney, *Men Who Have Walked With God,* p. 124.

[2] *Ibid.,* p. 124.

[3] *Ibid.,* p. 125.

not of prime importance. What was important, was to live and act nobly, in accord with the spirit.

He gathered many disciples who lived with him in a communal group, but unlike many groups of this kind, this one managed to live peaceably and successfully.

With him lived men and women of all walks of life and many orphaned children who were placed with him by their guardians. According to Porphyry, this community existed for the sole purpose of learning how to live so as "to rise to God and become one with Him."[4] Porphyry claims that four times during the time he was with Plotinus, the latter achieved this relationship with God, not as a mere passive mergence, but "by the ineffable act."[5]

During his lifetime, Plotinus was highly regarded, not only for his teachings, but for the quality of his life. In a day when even philosophers and teachers seemed to be marked by avarice and engaged in constant quarreling and vying for position, Plotinus earned a reputation for being at peace with himself, his fellow man, and God.

After his death in 270 A.D., Porphyry edited and published the *Enneads,* which were to change the course of Christian thought. St. Augustine, who completed the union of Christian theology and Greek philosophy, was profoundly influenced by Plotinus. Augustine could not accept Plato as he found him because he regarded Plato as incapable of separating the wheat from the chaff. He was delighted when he discovered a form of Platonism which seemed to combine the best of Greek and religious thought. Augustine is convinced that in Plotinus we have a perfect example of the disciple who has surpassed his master.

The reasons for this high evaluation of Plotinus by Augustine are not difficult to find. Both Plato and Plotinus were great thinkers. Of the two, Plato was the more original; but Plato stopped where Plotinus began.

To Plato, God was academic. There was a God, and God

---

4 *Ibid.,* p. 127.

5 *Ibid.,* p. 127.

could not be ignored, but Plato never claimed any firsthand knowledge or experience of God. In Platonic writings, God is spoken of in the same manner as truth, honesty, virtue, and justice. God is a concept rather than a person. Even if Plato were to regard God as a personality, he would have no warm feelings toward Him since God did not have a prominent place in Plato's life.

With Plotinus, this was not the case. God was known to Plotinus and entered into his thinking and life. God was the center of his life, and all else was trivial and unimportant.

The philosophic life, according to Plotinus, is the life that finds God. Ethics and morals will take care of themselves once man is brought into an active relationship with God. Plotinus makes it sound very easy, for he is convinced that the very nature of seeking God precludes lapses into evil conduct. If the individual is absorbed in seeking God, he will have time for little else.

Evil, according to Plotinus, is alien to man's true nature. Evil for the soul is tolerating that which is alien to its own nature.

Plotinus equates God with good, and uses the terms interchangeably. Yet, he does at times make a distinction between the two, and in one clear, succinct line sums up his philosophy; "Our business," he said, "is not merely to be sinless, but to be God."[6]

It is only thus, according to Plotinus, that the soul, which is united with the body at birth, can ultimately be free and have its real life with God. Pain results when the nature of the soul has been violated, and thus every sin brings as a consequence, pain to the soul of man.

The world is "derived" from God, and while it was divided off, imperfection crept in; yet, basically, it is beautiful. Plotinus did not feel in fellowship with the Christians who regarded this world with horror. For Plotinus, the universe is good, the world is good, and life is good. In this world, Plotinus says, "The Soul, caught up in that stream from the

---

[6] *Ibid.*, p. 130.

Divine, is awakened, suffused with a spiritual ecstacy, stirred by a new desire.[7]

This desire, if pursued, will bring the soul to God. But Plotinus is puzzled over the fact that the mystical experience does not last. He cannot comprehend why the soul, once it has risen to God, should always return to its former low level. But whatever the reason, and regardless of how frustrating, the soul must continually and forever seek oneness with God.

Plotinus does not chart a path to God, but instead, in the *Enneads,* the way is suggested haphazardly and incidentally.

We are told we must "disengage" from this world and seek God through contemplation. Purgation is easy once we embark on the spiritual road. The soul will find God, slip away, but return again and again. Each time the soul meets God, it returns but clinging to it is a certain purity. Each return brings the soul into a more perfect, Godlike state.

This is the process by which man goes on to perfection. The precept that has become a motto of the Neo-Platonists is, "Never did eye see the Sun unless first it had become Sunlike. Never can the soul see Primal Beauty unless itself be beautiful. Therefore, let each man become Godlike and beautiful who aspires to see Beauty and God."[8]

---

[7] *Ibid.,* p. 132.
[8] *Ibid.,* p. 142.

Chapter III
Dionysius the Areopogite

Sometime in the Fifth Century, a number of books appeared bearing the name of Dionysius and were assumed to be written by the same Dionysius who was converted by the Apostle Paul on the Aeropagus at Athens.

Most of the works were in the tradition of the Church Fathers, and hence, were received as one more body of works giving their support to the Catholic theology. According to legend, the Aeropogite was believed to be the first bishop of Athens and an evangelist to the City of Paris where he became a martyr to the Faith.

Among his works were a number of books on the Mystical theology, much influenced by Platonic thought. For over one thousand years, the books of Dionysius occupied a major place in Christian theology. Not only did they go further in setting forth the mystical teachings of Jesus and Paul, but they were a fusion of Greek and Hebrew thought and brought into Christianity a philosophical interpretation of the Faith.

Biographically, there is little that can be found concerning the Pseudo-Dionysius. He was, undoubtedly, a churchman, obscure enough to be able to write and circulate his writings without attracting much attention to himself. The little tract, *Concerning Mystical Theology,* is brief. It was written in Greek and had considerable circulation from the day it was produced and continued on through the "Dark Ages." In the middle of the Ninth Century, it was translated into Latin by Erigena or John the Scot, and from henceforth, it blazed a path across the sky of medieval Christian thought.[1]

It is unfortunate, in a way, that the author followed the pseudonymous tradition of the Hebrews. During the intense struggle in that period, three centuries before Christ, the Jews composed book after book of prophecy, each bearing the name of some traditional spiritual leader. Thus the authority of an

---

[1] Sheldon Cheney, *"Men Who Have Walked With God,"* p. 164.

earlier prophet was evoked for a new message given forth, so the author hoped, in his style and manner.

Hence, Dionysius, the author of *Concerning Mystical Theology,* is virtually untraceable. We detect in his writings, more of the Oriental abstraction than in the other Christian mystics, but then, we are not sure whether this expresses the influence of the writer or the Church of his time. The writings were in Greek, the language of half an Empire, but more significantly, he chose the name of a Greek convert. The neo-Platonic elements under those circumstances seemed to point toward a Greek, perhaps even a resident of Athens.

In a sense, this anonymity was fortunate, since for many centuries the writings of this writer carried the authority of apostolic tradition. In the confusion that accompanies the birth of any great religion, various writings appeared which distorted and even contradicted the religion of Jesus. Hence the Church authorities were confronted with the necessity of establishing some criteria or some authority for their teachings. The rule that was worked out was simple, and in an age of greater communication, might have been workable.

A book was considered to have authority if it was written by an apostle, or by one who knew an apostle. Thus the letters of Paul, Peter, James, and John became Scriptural, and the Gospels of Mark and Luke were recognized as cannonical because each had personal contact with the apostles . . . Mark with Paul and Barnabus, and Luke with the Apostle Peter.

The next group of books that were given a place of authority were the writings of the early Church Fathers. Most of them antedated the Council of Nicaea and included such names as Irenaeus, Hippolytus, Tertullian, Cyprian, Clement of Alexandria, and Origen.

Thus, Catholic doctrine was what the Scriptures said it was, and if anyone disagreed over an interpretation, he had only to turn to the Church Fathers for clarification. In general, this is the position of much of Christianity today, except that the major Church bodies add still another interpreter in the series . . . the Roman Church, Acquinas, the Lutheran,

The Book of Concord, the Anglican, Canon Law, and the Presbyterian, the Westminster Confession.

With this in mind, you can see the position of the pseudo-Dionysius. Only the later appearance of his writings (the Fifth Century) prevented their inclusion in the Canon of the Scriptures. His claim to know the apostles was unchallenged for centuries, and the influence of his books upon later Christian writers was without parallel.

What he taught was a happy combination of Greek and Christian thought. For him, to live is to be conscious of God. Evil emanates from ignorance of God. God is everywhere, yet transcendent and unknowable. He traced the steps of mysticism from an initial consciousness of God, followed by purification and rising to illumination and union.

Somewhat puzzling, however, is his description of the Union as a darkness of unknowing, or "Divine Darkness."[2] He seems to regard this stage as beyond the light.

His view of Jesus lacks the traditional warmth, and the humanity of Jesus is somewhat obscured. The Christ of Dionysius is quite remote and unapproachable. Nevertheless, he is Christocentric and dependent upon the revelation of Jesus Christ. Nor does he express anything but the orthodox view in any of his other books. Consequently, he was viewed as another of the Church Fathers, but who, because of his closeness to the Apostle Paul, did and could delve more deeply into the mysteries of the Faith.

He did, however, in good mystical tradition, indicate that much about God was unknown and unknowable. The very nature of God prevents us from adequately describing and defining Him. For, after all, to define is to limit, and God cannot be limited.

Like Lao-Tse, he, too, faces the paradox of the Tao, "If anyone, seeing God, knows what he sees, it is by no means God that he sees, but something created and knowable."[3]

---

[2] *Ibid.*, p. 165.

[3] *Ibid.*, p. 166.

In the best sense of the word, every mystic is an agnostic. He approaches as a skeptic, seeking proof, but paradoxically, before he finds the proof, he becomes a believer, convinced that logic compels us to eternally seek even though we may never find, or, if finding, never be able to tell about that which we have seen.

The mystic ultimately comes to the position where he no longer doubts the Ultimate Reality, but is equally convinced of the folly of believing that human sense can encompass every spiritual experience.

The works of Dionysius include, "On Celestial Hierarchy," "On Ecclesiastical Hierarchy," "On the Divine Names," and "On Mystical Theology." The two latter works are mystical in theology and heavily infused with Platonic philosophy.[4]

Like Johann Hamann, in the 18th Century, Dionysius becomes interested in the origin of language. To him, "It is in order to describe, discuss, and manage this common-sense universe that human language has been developed."[5]

Philology, in the hands of Dionysius, becomes a tool of theological research. Later we shall see that Johann Hamann would also use it as a tool for religious instruction.

Above all with Dionysius, we are confronted with the lonely, elusive and frustrating paradox of the mystical search.

"The simple, absolute and immutable mysteries of Divine Truth are hidden in the super-luminous darkness of that silence which revealeth in secret. For this darkness, though of deepest obscurity, is yet radiantly clear; and though beyond touch and sight, it more than fills our unseeing minds with splendors of transcendent beauty . . ."[6]

It is for the non-mystic, a babble of nonsense and confusion, but for those who have chosen to follow the path, the world of the Spirit described accurately, simply and with the utmost realism.

---

[4] Vergilius Ferm, Editor, "An Encyclopedia of Religion," p. 228.

[5] Aldous Huxley, "The Perennial Philosophy," p. 34.

[6] Ibid., pp. 33-34.

In the next few chapters we shall have to evaluate for ourselves what is real and what is illusion. The mystics we shall study will agree with Dionysius that the world of sense is treacherous and deceiving, and the obscurity of God is to be preferred to a mirage however clear the details or how fine the lines of the world held shimmering before our eyes.

Those who are impatient with the mystics insist that they should express themselves in more conventional language. However, this is not possible, for ordinary language cannot accurately describe extraordinary things.

For example, Eckhart uses, at one point, the mathematician's language to express exactly what he means. He says that God is equated with nothing.

Well, he doesn't mean that God doesn't exist, but with what can you equate God? Everything else is finite, God is infinite. God is unique. He is as Scotus Erigena phrases it, not a "what" but a That.

The world of the senses is easy to describe. It consists of a number of successive and presumably casually connected events. But the world of the spirit is beyond time and space and not a continuum. The difference is not one of degree but of dimension.

Dionysius would have us say not what God is, for this limits and tends to equate Him with finite things. But let us approach God, let us begin our search by stripping away that which He is not. He is not finite, He is not weakness, He is not limited, He is not capable of being encompassed by the human mind, He is not limited by time or space; in short, when we strip away the light of our knowledge, we see God in the darkness that remains.

He reveals in secret, in silence, in the deepest obscurity.

Chapter IV

Augustine
353-430

Few mystics ever hold high office of any kind. First, because they not only do not seek such offices, but more often, they avoid them. Second, because society as a whole does not trust the mystic, and he finds such offices closed to him.

Augustine, a native of North Africa, was one of the few exceptions, and his career is equally unusual and different.

He was born in 354[1] of a Christian woman and a pagan father. His parents were in comfortable circumstances, though not wealthy. He received a good education, and chose his father's pagan way of life.

At 17, he acquired a concubine by whom he had a son, Adeodatus.[2] At the age of 19, the study of Cicero's HORTENSIUS produced a partial conversion, and he began to study the Scriptures.[3]

He turned to the Manichaeistic sect to which he remained faithful for nine years. He lived partly in Carthage and partly in Tagaste where he engaged in study and teaching. At Carthage, he was honored for the production of a theatrical poem. He achieved some success as a Manichaean teacher, but at the height of his success, disillusionment set in. His friends noticed his intellectual doubting and urged him to see and discuss his doubts with Faustus, the most highly respected Manichaean leader of his day. His meeting with Faustus had the opposite effect of which his friends had sought, and he was completely disillusioned; and while outwardly remaining a Manichaean, he now, inwardly, was a skeptic.[4]

In 383, he moved to Rome where he obtained a government appointment as a teacher of rhetoric in Milan—then the Western capitol of the Empire.

---

1 Williston Walker, "*A History of the Christian Church,*" p. 175.
2 *Ibid.,* p. 176.
3 *Ibid.,* p. 176.
4 *Ibid.,* p. 176.

In Milan, Augustine came under the powerful preaching of Ambrose, whom he went to hear in order to study his style of preaching. No change was made in his religious affiliation though he was much interested in the skeptical philosophy of the New Academy.

His mother, Monica, joined him and persuaded him to become betrothed. He did this partially to please his mother and partially because it fitted his new station in life. He dismissed his concubine and entered into a less creditable relation with another.

At this point in life, he came in contact with Neo-Platonism through the translations of Victorinus.[5] The combination of Plato's writings and Ambrose's preachings began to produce an acute uneasiness in Augustine.

In Manichaean teaching, evil was pictured as having a positive existence, and while not desirable, was at least real. Now he saw the spiritual world as the only real world and in God, the source of all good; but more important, all reality.

The cleavage between his immoral life and his new ideals began to make him uncomfortable.

A traveled African, Pontitianus, told him of the hermit monks that lived in Egypt and of the quality of life they lived. It bothered Augustine that unlearned men could apparently live a moral life, and a man as learned as he was could not resist temptation. The more he thought about it, the more discontented he became. Finally, he heard the voice of a child from a neighboring house say, "Take up and read," and he reached for a copy of the epistles, and his eyes fell on the the words: "Not in rioting and drunkenness, not in chambering and wantonness, not in strife and envying; but put ye on the Lord Jesus Christ, and make not provision for the flesh to fulfill the lusts thereof."[6] It produced a profound conviction and a new, changed Augustine emerged.

---

[5] *Ibid.*, p. 177.

[6] *Ibid.*, p. 177.

The change occurred in the late summer of 386, making him 33 years of age. The Freudians have had a great time with this, arguing that he was burned out at this early age and hence, found it comparatively easy to put behind him the lusts of the flesh. Since most of us are relatively mature, I'm sure we no longer regard anyone at 33 as being too old to sin.

Much has been written about Augustine, and he has more interpreters than almost any other spiritual figure. The key to an understanding of Augustine is the "Confessions" which remains a monument of spiritual autobiography.

The century which had preceded Augustine's, had produced no great spiritual monument. It had, instead, attempted to define God in so precise a terminology as to make Him seem cold and remote. Men could be inspired by a personal God, but it is difficult to see any great inspiration proceeding from the Nicene Creed.

Augustine restored to the Christian Church the idea that God was personally connected with man. When he thought of God philosophically, it was in terms borrowed from Neo-Platonism, but when he thought of God as a person who had transformed him and made him whole, his terminology was simple, warm and almost familiar.

The reality of God is the one certainty. God is real because Augustine speaks with Him every day. Two things seem real, dreadfully, awfully real to Augustine. His sins he cannot face, he cannot deny, and he cannot erase. Yet, there is a God that can and does redeem man and Augustine, in particular, from his iniquity.

Augustine is a great mystical contradiction. He "explains" God when he is engaged in abstract and academic discussion, especially in his controversies with the Donatists and the Pelagians; but when he speaks of the God whom he knows from experience, he finds words inadequate; and like the mystics who followed him, draws back from the task.

Describing one brief contemplative experience, Augustine says, "My mind withdrew its thoughts from experience, extracting itself from the contradictory throng of sensuous images, that it might find out what that light was wherein it

27

was bathed . . . And thus, with the flash of one hurried glance, it attained to the vision of THAT WHICH IS. And then, at last, I saw Thy invisible things understood by means of the things that are made, but I could not sustain my gaze; my weakness was dashed back, and I was relegated to my ordinary experience, bearing with me only a loving memory, and as it were, the fragrance of those desirable meats on the which, as yet, I was not able to feed."[7]

In his more conventional writings, he attempts more detailed descriptions of God and of religious experience. Here, he can only refer to his experience as a "fragrance" and at that, something that he possessed only for a moment. Yet, this moment is but a portion of the Pearl of Great Price. Again and again do the mystics seek this experience. It inspires them sustains them, and is their fulfillment. All their hopes, their aspirations, and their desires are fulfilled in such moments as these.

If the Bishop of Hippo deems it important, nay claims —this is the reason, the explanation for all that he is and desires to become, can anyone cast it aside as of trivial worth? If this is the source of their strength, their productivity, and their creativeness, whether a delusion or a reality, it must be studied and evaluated.

In Augustine, we have the curious mixture of mystic and theologian. In Book I of the "Confessions," he described God in these terms: "What art Thou then, my God? For who is Lord but the Lord? Or who is God save our God? Most highest, most good, most potent, most omnipotent; most merciful, yet most just; most hidden, yet most present; most beautiful, yet most strong; stable, yet incomprehensible; unchangeable, yet all-changing; never new, never old; all-renewing, and bring age upon the proud, and they know it not; ever working, ever at rest; still gathering, yet nothing lacking; supporting, filling, and overspreading; creating, nourishing, and maturing; seeking, yet having all things. Thou lovest, without passion; art jealous, without anxiety; repentest, yet grievest not; art

---

[7] *Evelyn Underhill,* p. 331.

angry, yet serene; changest Thy works, Thy purpose unchanged; receivest again what Thou findest, yet didst never lose; never in need, yet rejoicing in gains; never covetous, yet exacting usury. Thou receivest over and above, that Thou mayest owe; and who hath aught that is not Thine? Thou payest debts, owing nothing; remittest debts, losing nothing. And what had I now said, my God, my life, my holy joy? Or what saith any man when he speaks of Thee? Yet woe to him that speaketh not, since mute are even the most eloquent."[8]

The classic attributes of God stated, enumerated and dry as dust—but something else is here—God is also incomprehensible, and whatever man says about Him amounts to nothing. Man speaks of God only because he dares not remain mute; for even silence has something to say.

More typical of the mystic is this passage:

"Where hast Thou not walked with me, O Truth, instructing me what to beware, and what to desire? Thou art the abiding Light, which I consulted, and heard Thee directing and commanding me; nor in all these matters can I find any safe place for my soul except in Thee, to Whom I am gathered, and nothing apart. And sometimes, Thou admittest me to a wondrous love, in my inmost soul; rising to a strange sweetness, which, if it were perfected in me, I know not how it might be different from the Eternal Life."[9]

God is here, not speculated upon, but experienced. How and in what manner Augustine does not always attempt to say, but since his awakening, he constantly feels God pulling him in one direction even as his passions pull him in another.

In his words, "And being then admonished to return to myself, I entered even into my inward self, Thou being my Guide: and able I was, for Thou wert become my Helper. And I entered and beheld with the eye of my soul, above my mind, the Light Unchangeable. Not this ordinary light, which all my flesh may look upon, nor as it were, a greater of the

---

[8] Edward Pusey, trans., "The Confessions of St. Augustine," p. 3.
[9] Sheldon Cheney, "Men Who Have Walked With God," p. 162.

29

same kind, as though the brightness of this should be manifold brighter, and with its greatness, take up all space. Not such was this light, but other, yea, far other from these. Nor was it above my soul, as oil is above water, nor yet as heaven above earth: but above to my soul, because It made me; and I below It, because I was made by It. He that knows the Truth, knows what that light is; and he that knows It, knows eternity. Love knoweth it. O Truth Who art Eternity! And Love, Who art Truth! And Eternity, Who art Love! Thou art my God, to Thee do I sigh night and day. Thee when I first knew, Thou liftedst me up, that I might see there was what I might see, and that I was not yet such as to see. And Thou didst beat back the weakness of my sight, streaming forth Thy beams of Light upon me most strongly, and I trembled with love and awe: and I perceived myself to be far off from Thee, in the region of unlikeness, as if I heard this Thy voice from on high: 'I am the food of grown men, grow, and thou shalt feed upon Me; nor shalt thou convert Me, like the food of thy flesh into thee, but thou shalt be converted into Me.' And I learned, that Thou for iniquity chastenest man, and Thou madest my soul to consume away like a spider. And I said, 'Is Truth therefore nothing because it is not diffused through space finite or infinite?' And Thou criest to me from afar: 'Yet verily, I AM that I AM.' And I heard, as the heart heareth, nor had I room to doubt, and I would sooner doubt that I live than that Truth is not, which is clearly seen, being understood by those things which are made."[10]

In this and similar passages, Augustine places knowledge of truth beyond reason, just as he held that man's intelligence could not aid him to ethical conduct. He distrusted the intellect as a guide to the highest good. Therefore, man must found his life upon God. God's Will must become my will. His intelligence must become, and can become, my intelligence. God's Will cannot be discovered by reason. The only way to God's Will is by contemplation and illumination. All men, however, are not capable of receiving illumination

---

[10] Pusey, trans., Augustine's "Confessions," pp. 117-118.

direct from God, so for them, the institution of the Church provides it second hand.

The function of reason in Augustine's philosophy is not to interpret truth, but rather to attempt to understand revealed truth. This was the portion of Augustine's teachings that the Church best understood, and the Middle Ages became scholastic and attempted to explain all the church dogma with a series of intellectual gymnastics. The experiences of Augustine were little understood, but tolerated as the divine means of producing a convenient and desirable conversion.

However, this is not a precise road, that is subject to ecclesiastical control, and hence, not to be stressed or encouraged among the mass of churchgoers.

With Augustine, mysticism is firmly established in the Church. If anyone in the next thousand years doubted Augustine or questioned his theology, there was the authority of none less than Dionysius, a convert of Paul, who pictured God in the same experiential terms. When the mistake regarding the identity of Dionysius is discovered, it is Augustine whose greatness and authority gives support and orthodoxy to Dionysius.

Chapter V

Meister Eckhart

"He wished to know more than he should!" With those words Pope John XXII condemned Meister Eckhart a heretic. Yet Eckhart had been the most popular preacher of his day, his sermons were widely read, and throughout his life he had held posts of responsibility in the Dominican order. But not until after his death was he finally convicted of heresy.

His preaching was unusual and explored theological depths few preachers would attempt to talk upon today. He spoke in a rude, ignorant age, yet his Church was crowded with both uneducated and educated people alike.

Eckhart thought of himself as an orthodox son of the Church, yet the casual study of his sermons reveals a wide divergence between the ideas of Eckhart and the prevailing view held in the Church of his day.

It is not startling that Eckhart was convicted of heresy; rather it is difficult to understand how he escaped trial and conviction for so many years of his life. Had he been an obscure and unknown priest, as was Dionysius, we might understand, but Eckhart had a distinguished career and had taken part in many of the great controversies of his day.

Johannes Eckhart was born about 1260 in Hochheim, a small village in Germany. The biographical details of his life are almost lost, only fragments of his sermons and books remain. It was probably in his fifteenth year that he enrolled in the Dominican monastery in Erfurt. At the time, at least nine years' study was required, and somewhere near the year 1300, he is referred to as "Brother Eckhart," "Prior of Erfurt," "Vicar of Thuringia."

His talents evidently were recognized early. During this period, he published a pamphlet known as "Talks of Instruction." This little book consists of talks or sermons concerning prayer, self-denial, growth, and other topics concerning the spiritual life. It has been said that in these talks, Eckhart did not go beyond the range of Catholic piety of his time. Yet there is an earnestness and devotion that did go beyond that of the average ecclesiastical office holder.

In 1300 the Dominicans sent Eckhart to college in Paris on a teaching mission. It should be noted here that, as a member of the Dominican order, Eckhart not only enjoyed serving in one of the most influential factions in the Church, but by his identification with the Dominicans, he automatically became involved in the most heated kind of ecclesiastical politics. The other prominent Catholic order, the Franciscans, competed for power and publicity. Most of the bickering was about theology, but underneath lay some very untheological envy and lust for power.

We know little of Eckhart's visit to Paris beyond the fact that the College of Paris conferred on him the Licentiate and Master's Degree. He evidently made a profound impression upon those in academic circles. Henceforth, he was known as Meister Eckhart. About 1307, the duties of Vicar of Bohemia were added to his position as Provincial of the Dominican order in Saxony. Thus, at the time when Eckhart was doing the most writing, he held posts which involved extensive travel and much hard and routine work. This is not unusual for people of mystical genius, but seems to be typical. They are people who often seem to spread themselves thin, and carry tremendous loads of responsibility. We are not certain whether they are able to carry these responsibilities because of their illumination, or whether the load of their responsibilities helps bring on the illumination. Probably, it works both ways. It was at this time that he wrote, "The Book of Divine Comfort," said to have been written for the Queen of Hungary who was much in need of courage and spiritual help. This book is one of the finest expositions of the idea of God as Father. In it Eckhart shows the close relationship between man and God, while decisively demonstrating the great gulf between creator and creature. To Eckhart, the gulf is very wide, but in that one word, "Father," he has found an effective bridge over the gulf.

Now the idea of God as Father is as old as Christianity itself, as are all the ideas which Eckhart expressed. Stated boldly, Eckhart's ideas do not seem any different than those expressed by the Church of his own day. Yet, Eckhart soon found himself charged with heresy. It was heresy not of idea but of degree. To state that God is Father meant to Eckhart that God and man (man in a limited sense) are of the same genus. This "little spark" of God needed only to be fanned into a living flame. The next logical step is to state the doctrine of the priesthood of all believers. Eckhart formulated a doctrine that was to find its way into the Reformation via "Theologia Germanica," a book later to be written by one of his followers but which went further than Luther and the Reformers cared to follow.

For what Eckhart stated was not simply that man could approach God directly, without an intermediary, but that man could become one with God. "I became man for you. If you do not become God for me, you do me wrong."[1]

The Church as an institution saw a threat to its existence; for this idea seemed to leave no room for the Church as an intermediary between God and man. This alone might not have brought about his trial for heresy, but two factors contributed to his trial and ultimate conviction. The first was his affiliation with the Dominicans. As a noted Dominican, he was bound to become the target of the rival Franciscan Order. There are always those who feel that, if they can blacken the name of one of the members of the opposing party, they can discredit the entire organization. The Archbishop of Cologne, who was Eckhart's superior and a Franciscan, turned loose two other Franciscans to investigate Eckhart. These two bloodhounds managed to turn up numerous pamphlets and sermons from which they drew a long list of alleged errors.

The second factor which conspired to bring about the charge of heresy was his popularity as a preacher. His Church was crowded with simple and learned folk alike. It is not surprising that many of those who attended his services belonged to wild religious movements bordering on the lunatic fringe. A popular preacher attracts all sorts and manner of people from the very orthodox to the most heretical of men.

Specifically, there was the Beghard movement, noted more for its zeal than for its soundness of doctrine. Eckhart

---

[1] Evelyn Underhill, *"Mysticism,"* pp. 419-420.

cannot be identified with the movement, but he undoubtedly regarded them with sympathy even though he must have shied away from their excesses.

Yet, Eckhart's popularity with these people was regarded with suspicion, since the Church was doing much to stamp out bizarre religious movements.

The charge of heresy came as a shock to Eckhart, for he had never entertained any doubts concerning his theological orthodoxy. Yet, when it did come about, he was willing enough to consider the possibility that in a narrow, literal sense, he might be unorthodox. He stated, "I may err, but I may not be a heretic—for the first has to do with the mind, and the second, with the will!"

Unlike Augustine, it was not his liking to quarrel over theology—he preferred to think that the indwelling of the Divine within each man was not dependent on precise theological definition. Perhaps this indifference to theological niceties was the heresy that theologically oriented churchmen could not tolerate. He was reluctant in his preaching to attempt to reach men through argument, for like Augustine, he felt strongly that reason was limited. He chose, instead, to share his experiences with God and thus bring men to a knowledge of Him.

In January, 1327, he appeared at the Archbishop's court at Cologne to defend himself. In a sermon, a few weeks later, he defended his faith and stated that he had avoided all errors, but if proven erroneous, would retract. This challenge to debate was not accepted, and on February 22, 1327, his appeal to Rome was denied. History gives us little concerning the next events, but he was condemned posthumously in the bull of John XXII dated March 27, 1329.

It was, perhaps, well for Eckhart that he passed away before John issued his bull condemning him. For, regardless of what the Church might have had in store for him, Eckhart would have regarded the bull as a bitter pill. The Church had been his life. He had dedicated himself to the Church, had given his best to her, and probably his only error was his desire to know God better than the men of his time.

Many of the mystics cannot be understood unless one

reads all of their works. But with Eckhart, it is much more simple. In a sermon which a disciple has entitled, "This is Meister Eckhart from whom God hid nothing," we have the gist of this 14th Century mystic's teachings.

Speaking of Christ's birth, he states that "St. Augustine says that this birth is always happening. And yet, if it does not occur in me, how could it help me? Everything depends on that."[2]

Does the Catholic Church have room for more than one Christ? Throughout its history and through every document of every branch of the Church is the insistence that Jesus Christ is unique. But Eckhart goes on to say, "Not only the Son of the heavenly Father is born in the darkness which is his own, but you, too, are born there, a son of the same heavenly Father, and to you, also, he gives power."[3]

And the final and conclusive claim to be co-equal with God appears at the end of the above quoted sermon: "May God, newly born in human form, eternally help us that we frail people being born in Him, may be Divine. Amen."[4]

Isn't this crystal clear that Eckhart believes that all may become Christs? Jesus did not come into the world to be unique but to lead the way. The way is to God, to dwell in Him and He in us. We, according to Eckhart, are meant to become Divine.

When Eckhart denied that he was a heretic, he merely betrayed his inability to understand how seriously the Church regarded its own doctrinal and dogmatic formulas. Had he been given the opportunity, Eckhart might have quoted Christ, especially the 17th Chapter of St. John, to defend his position. But he wasn't given the opportunity, and he was to have soon learned that the Church, while it professes to make Scripture the rule of faith, interprets Scripture according to the formulas worked out by the builders of scholastic and reformation theology. Eckhart was condemned

---

[2] Raymond B. Blakney's translation, *"Meister Eckhart,"* p. 95.

[3] *Ibid.,* p. 102.

[4] *Ibid.,* p. 102.

by the ancient Catholic Church, but he would also be condemned by the modern Catholic Church and the Protestants oriented toward Reformation and neo-orthodox theology.

This is the challenge of Eckhart, "Would you be a Christ?" To understand it is one thing, to do it, quite another. Perhaps the Friends of God, Tauler and Suso, will show us the way.

Chapter VI

Suso, Tauler, and The Friends of God

In Eckhart's sermon, "Eternal Birth," we have the "how" of illumination. We "must depart from all crowds and go back to the starting point, the course (of the soul) out of which (we) came . . . (we must leave them all: sense perception, imagination, and all that (we) discover in self or intend to do . . . After that, (we) may experience this birth —but otherwise not."[1]

We cannot, insists Eckhart, experience this birth by any avenue of the senses. Ideas of God, "for example, that God is good, wise, merciful, or whatever ideas that are creatures of the reason, and yet divine,"[2] will in no wise bring man to the divine birth.

"This work (birth), when it is perfect, will be due solely to God's action while you have been passive."[3] Once we have prepared ourselves for God's coming, through the awakening and purging process, there is little else we can do but wait for His presence to steal into our soul "like a thief in the night." In a sense, it comes as much from within as without, since Eckhart believes that the soul is nothing more or less than a portion of the Divine essence.

We can prepare ourselves in many ways, but to Eckhart, the most important factor is detachment of self-negation, in German, "Abgeschiedenheit." This includes both seclusion of self from the world and also the forsaking of self. Man needs nothing so much as to escape from his ever-present self, or perhaps his awareness of self or self-awareness. Perhaps we can think of it as a man's need to stand free of himself.

He will do this, not by giving obedience in the medieval sense, but through love. Perfect love, according to the

---

[1] Raymond B. Blakney's translation, *"Meister Eckhart,"* p. 118.

[2] *Ibid.,* p. 118.

[3] *Ibid.,* p. 119.

German mystics, seeks to return to God a small portion of the love He has shown to us. He reaches out for us with a love that Eckhart compares to a fisherman's hook; once we are caught, we are drawn to Him, and there is no escaping.

Over and over the mystics tell us that man cannot bring about His illumination. This comes without effort to those who have prepared themselves to receive God. Stated in its most simple form, Jesus said, "The pure in heart shall see God."

The German mystics experienced visions of God and His mysteries which they described in a bewildering variety of ways. However, they all had the following common characteristics:

First, these illuminations came suddenly and without warning. The individual felt as if he was immersed in the Divine essence, as if God had surrounded him. To some, it was described as being bathed in warmth, and by others, as a fragrance.

This feeling is accompanied by an ecstasy in which the individual feels joy, assurance, and a sense of being a part of the entire universe.

In every case, the mystic emerges as one who no longer knows in the intellectual sense, but trades his intellectual knowledge for an intuitive knowledge. The mystics feel that to know God with the mind, through either inductive or deductive reasoning, is a second-hand knowledge compared to the "knowing" that they experienced in these brief states of illumination.

Before he knew God in a fragmented sense, but in the state of illumination he "saw" God WHOLE. Here is his greatest stumbling block since what he experienced is too great, such a vast conception that it eludes the ordinary imagination. He saw only that which the limited, finite mind can see, he grasped only a small fragment of what he saw. In the process, there was an awareness of something beyond the capacity of the mind.

In no case, have any of the mystics felt capable of describing adequately the nature of their experiences. If the mind has limitations, language imposes still further limitations. Also, the mind grasped infinitely more than it is capable of communicating to others.

With this experience comes a sense of immortality, and fear of death vanishes for once and for all time.

For some of the mystics, these experiences brought a new attitude toward sin. As we know, all of them, once they experienced an awakening, were haunted and even driven to extreme forms of asceticism in an effort to purge themselves of their sins.

During the periods of illumination, this sense of sin falls away, and the mystic ceases to feel its weight. By this, I do not merely mean to say that they feel forgiven or that they feel no longer tempted. The sensation is almost as if the mystic no longer sees that sin exists.

Except for certain periods, sometimes described as the dark night of the soul, the mystic never wrestles with sin again. The whole world rests more easily upon his shoulders, and a certain lightness of manner, which men have found charming and sometimes irritating, marks their characters.

Most had an evenness of temperament that was quite remarkable, but some, like Heinrich Suso, alternated between an ecstatic bliss and a brooding torment called the "dark night of the soul." He told of an illumination at the age of eight, and spoke often of visions in which he "tasted the bliss of Eternal Life." He claimed he saw Sophia, "The Heavenly Wisdom," and thus helped give impetus to the Sophia idea which already had caught the imagination of the Friends of God, the Brothers of the Free Spirit, and similar mystical groups.

Closely associated with Suso was Johannes Tauler, also a Dominican, and a friend of Meister Eckhart. It was Tauler, rather than Eckhart and Suso, who was closely identified with the Friends of God.

The Friends of God was a movement of people who did not aspire to an organization, but which met throughout Europe and shared certain aims and characteristics. Tauler laid down certain marks for the Friends of God, and they tell us something of the group:

1. They offered themselves out of pure love as a living sacrifice to God.

2. They were persistent in what they would do for God, knowing that nothing great could be accomplished in the short time of a few years.

3. Neighbors should not be judged: "I would prefer to bite my tongue than to judge a person. Leave your neighbor to God and judge yourself."

4. They should have peace; yet also a restlessness to know more of God.

5. Moderation rather than asceticism is the true way of religious living.

6. Suffering is the greatest index into a Christian: "A soul full of God and a natural body full of suffering is the inheritance of the Friends of God. Our Lord will not leave any of His friends without suffering."[4]

These Gottesfreunde banded together in small meetings where they prayed together and studied and circulated the mystical literature produced by Eckhart, Suso, Tauler, and many unknown authors.

These people represented all walks of life and were both in and out of the Church. The one common characteristic was to seek God and befriend Him. When they sought to find Him, it was in the immediate personal way of the mystics. In one way or another, they all felt that they knew God; but more important, they expected someday to know Him better.

Illumination was expected, and because it was expected, it came to many. They discussed these illuminations in the same manner that men discuss other experiences. They did so without boasting, seeking only to share with others the mysteries and the joy that was to be found by walking with God.

These people were not seeking after signs, nor were they content with ecstatic experiences that led nowhere. They

---

[4] Thomas S. Kepler, editor, "*Theologia Germanica,*" The World Publishing Co., New York, 1952, pp. 23-24.

sincerely sought and expected to achieve a union with God.

They lived in an age when such union could be discussed and even preached about from the leading pulpits of the land. One of these pulpits was occupied by Johann Tauler who preached at Strasburg and was generally regarded as the leader of the Friends of God.

During this time, he preached a sermon entitled, "Union with God," which is one of the simplest and best descriptions of the changes that take place within a man who experiences such a union.

Tauler feels he is on solid theological ground in this sermon on "Union with God" since he claims that St. Paul had attained this union, and as a proof text he quotes St. Paul when he said, "And I live, now not I, but Christ liveth in me." (Gal. 2:20)[5]

What St. Paul has done we also can do according to Tauler, but the first requirement is that we lose ourselves and forget ourselves. As long as man is self-conscious or conscious of self, he cannot have God.

Union is precisely what the name implies and permits no multiplicity of persons. In a sense, every creature has come forth *from this* unity and yearns to return to it. The soul, however, cannot return until it can cast free of the self in which it was lodged at birth. Tauler says what Christ said before him, that the soul had a prior existence before this life. "Every creature comes forth from this unity by an immediate creative act, and each one tends again to be absorbed in its entire existence into indivisible unity, according to each one's capability."[6]

The soul, then, is nothing less than a portion of that Divine Unity. By a peculiar alchemy, it has become lodged in the physical self and is constantly threatened by this self. Life is a struggle to determine whether the fleshly self will absorb the soul or whether the soul will overcome the flesh and fashion into the likeness of God.

---

[5] Gilmore & Scott, editors, "*World's Devotional Classics,*" Volume III, Funk & Wagnalls Co., New York, 1916, p. 99.

[6] *Ibid.,* p. 100.

Until the soul is free of the body, that is, gains victory over it, it cannot be reunited with God. But the soul that unites with God is not that soul which was, but a new, stronger and more vital part of the Divine Essence.

It becomes something greater and larger than it was, through the struggle to gain its freedom from the fleshly lusts that war against it.

"The more the soul's powers are detached from outward things and gathered into one in the interior life, all the stronger grows God's action inwardly, and all the diviner and more perfect."[7] It is for this that we have been created, and it is for Him that we shall live. Like Christ, we must die to self and rise again that death shall no more have dominion over us.

Until this self is transformed and united with the soul and lost in the soul, it cannot become one with God. All mental and spiritual activity must flow in the direction of God, and only when we reach Him shall we find rest and tranquility.

While we must shun company that would turn us from the direction of God, Tauler warns that we must not separate into little sects. The only thing that should separate us from others is the quality of our lives and the depth of our love for God.

Thus the Friends of God came together not to separate themselves from the world, but to give one another mutual encouragement and help. Without organization or recognized leaders, the group died out when the Reformation froze religious thinking and religious expression into rigid patterns, Roman Catholic and Protestant.

It was not the repression of dissident groups that was primarily responsible, but the tendency of the Reformation to consume the religious energies of the Age in controversy and the erection of theological systems. The lover of God was replaced by the explainer of God, and the experience of illumination by conversion to a particular system of theology.

---

[7] *Ibid.,* p. 101.

Men no longer became awakened but converted to this or that theological or ecclesiastical system.

More important, perhaps, is the fact that the Reformation made men afraid of religious experience. The man who had experiences of illumination or saw visions was unpredictable in an age when men demanded to know who was a friend and who was an enemy. Men felt compelled to declare themselves as belonging to one camp or another. Their identification with either Calvinism, Lutheranism, or Romanism left little room for anything else. Men became not God centered, but system centered, and the life of the mystical movement ebbed away, almost unnoticed.

Oddly enough, it was Luther who gave new prominance to THEOLOGICA GERMANICA, one of the Literary masterpieces of the Friends of God, and the Reformation in England unleashed a new and tremendously vital mystical movement in 17th Century England.

Chapter VII

Theologia Germanica

With the work of Thomas Aquinas, the Church entered into a new phase of history, high scholasticism. The aim of theological study was to give knowledge of God. The scholastic method was the exploration of the world of sense and reason, but it was not limited to reason.

According to Aquinas, reason was not sufficient but needed the added help of revelation. Unfortunately, revelation was bound to the Fathers, the interpretations of the councils, and the living authority of the Church.

In sharp contrast to the world of Aquinas is THEOLOGIA GERMANICA, which opens with the statement that the imperfect, that is, man and his finite reason, can never comprehend the perfect. Before man can know God, he must separate himself from everything that makes him man, including his dependence upon reason.

Man must stand aside from himself since "Sin is nought else, but that the creature turneth away from the unchangeable God and betaketh itself to the changeable; that is to say, that it turneth away from the Perfect, to 'that which is in part' and imperfect, and most often to itself."[1]

Man has gone astray by setting up a claim to a small portion of God's universe. In declaring himself a free spirit, man has divorced himself from God. God, it is true, wants man to come to Him because he may, rather than because he must. Yet, man must not mistake this liberty to live apart from God as being without price. It is liberty to go to hell, for the saint realizes that life apart from God is not only hell, but the *only* hell there is.

The author interprets Adam's Fall from the traditional pessimistic point of view but states that the sin is not an act of disobedience but man's "claiming something for his own, and because of his I, Mine, Me, and the like."[2]

---

[1] *"Theologia Germanica,"* p. 39.
[2] *Ibid.,* p. 40.

In the third chapter is the raison d'te of the Friends of God. The Creator and the Created are eternally bound together because, "I cannot do the work (heal the breach caused by the Fall) without God, and God may not or will not without me: for it shall be accomplished, in me, too, God must be made man."[3]

As Christ had two natures, or two eyes, so has man. One has "the power of seeing into eternity, the other of seeing into time and the creatures."[4]

Obviously, man, like Christ, must spend some time in deciding which eye he will serve, for no man can have two masters. But the significant thing about THEOLOGIA GERMANICA is the manner in which it places ordinary man on a par with Christ, yea, with God. In a time when the uniqueness of Christ was the essence of orthodoxy, this author dared to say what was possible for Jesus is possible for all men.

The author admits that it is commonly denied for the soul "while it is yet in the body, to reach so high as to cast a glance into eternity, and receive a foretaste of eternal life and eternal blessedness."[5] Though it may be denied, the author cites an authority who says that it is possible. The authority cited is St. Dionysius, and though we know that their basis for regarding him as an authority was a blunder, in the Fourteenth Century no one questioned it.

The author quotes Dionysius as saying, "For the beholding of the hidden things of God, shalt thou forsake sense and the things of the flesh, and all that the sense can apprehend, and that reason of her own powers can bring forth, and all things created and uncreated that reason is able to comprehend and know and shalt take thy stand upon an utter abandonment of thyself, and as knowing none of the aforesaid things, and enter into union with Him who is, and who is above all existence and all knowledge."[6]

---

[3] *Ibid.*, p. 41.

[4] *Ibid.*, p. 49.

[5] *Ibid.*, p. 51.

[6] *Ibid.*, 51-52.

Here in a capsule is the mystical theology which the author of THEOLOGIA GERMANICA expounds. It cannot be challenged or doubted "For does not Paul's convert say exactly the same thing?" Like Augustine before him, the author moves with confidence and the assurance that what he is saying is orthodox and backed by the highest and greatest apostolic authority. Only the words of one of the original twelve would have carried greater weight.

How or in what manner a man sees the Kingdom of Heaven is not explained, but according to the author, "a single one of these excellent glances is better, worthier, higher and more pleasing to God, than all that the creature can perform as a creature.[7]

Yet, before man can perceive heaven, he must of necessity perceive hell. During the state of purgation, a man feels that all of creation must rise up against him, and scorn him because of the enormity of his sin. I like the thought that the author has, that as long as a man is either in heaven or in hell, he is safe. It is only when he is neither contemplating the bliss of heaven nor the enormity of his sin that he is in danger of succumbing to the creature comforts of this world. Such a man, says the author, wavers hither and thither, not knowing what manner of man that he is.

The author of the book is by no means the hermit type that many men believe mystics to be. He cautions in Chapter XIII against going it alone. He quotes Tauler as saying that many men falsely believe themselves capable of going ahead before they have completed their instruction from others and from literature, and moving on before they are able to "understand the truth aright."[8] Our author urges that the awakened individual remember that "no one can be made perfect in a day."[9] He urges him to walk with other like-minded men and women and receive from them instructions, reproof, counsel, and teaching. The Friends of God were a close and intimate fellowship. They believed that no man came to God by

---

7 *Ibid.*, p. 52.
8 *Ibid.*, p. 66.
9 *Ibid.*, p. 66.

himself, but was expected to come to God hand in hand with a brother.

Man was led upward to God in three stages. He must be cleansed, that is, purged, he must be enlightened, and there must be a union.

The purging comes by three states, by contrition and sorrow for sin, by full confession, and by hearty amendment.

The enlightenment comes by eschewal of sin, by the practice of virtue and good works, and by the willing endurance of all manner of temptation and trials.

The union comes to those who are perfect and who have taken three steps.

They have achieved pureness and singleness of heart, and perfect love by contemplation of God, or the practice of the presence of God.

About the latter, the author warns that no man comes to God by such questioning or reading. The way demands of man an absolute renunciation of himself. "So long as a man clingeth unto the elements and fragments of this world (and above all to himself,) and holdeth converse with them, and maketh great account of them, he is deceived and blinded, and perceiveth what is good no further than as it is most convenient and pleasant to himself and profitable to his own ends.[10]

We are to forsake all things, stand aside from ourselves, and respond to God's will. Having resigned ourselves completely to the Will of God, God moves towards us and we become united in soul.

The union as defined by the author is this: "It is that we should be of a truth purely, simply, and wholly at one with the One Eternal Will of God, or altogether without will, so that the created will should flow out in the Eternal Will, and be swallowed up and lost therein, so that the Eternal Will alone should do and leave undone in us.[11]

Nothing that we can do will bring this about, except our renunciation of the world.

---

[10] *Ibid.*, p. 81.

[11] *Ibid.*, p. 103.

We back away from the world and bump into God. He comes to live at ease with His Creator. In a sense, he no longer concerns himself with custom, order, law, and precepts, not because he lives outside of these, but because living for him has become harmonious with the cosmic forces of life. Nothing is forced, artificial or "according to the rule," but flows easily at one with the Spirit of God.

Such a man is made perfect in love, and has no difficulty loving all of God's creatures. The man living under the law, struggling through the state of purgation, must fight to love all men, but after union, it comes without effort, indeed, it would be an effort not to love even one of God's creatures.

The author recognizes the danger of self-deception in all this and devotes many chapters dealing with the true and the false union. The gist of it is, that if it is of God, the man who experiences this union seeks nothing for himself. He gives not the glory to himself for his own sake, but for the love which he bestows upon others. There is no turning in upon oneself. Narcissus committed the greatest sin. God and His friends love all things, and it must be admitted one must truly love oneself, but not for one's own sake. This is an outgoing love, and a creature of God loves the things that he can do for others. Pride is the sin of the spiritual man and the Pascal paradox is the threat to all seekers of God.

Pascal struggled and struggled for humility only to discover that he became proud of being humble. So men who struggle to achieve the humility necessary that God may come and dwell in their souls may lose Him because of their pride in their achievement. Once this union has been achieved, no man may lose Him except through pride.

Chapter VIII
The Cloud of Unknowing

If the light of mysticism burned bright on the Continent of Europe, it shone fully as brightly on the British Isles. For some reason, the world seldom thinks of the British as being inclined towards mysticism, and yet, from age to age, Great Britain has seen more mystics than probably any other nation, including Germany.

In the Fourteenth Century, Julian of Norwich, Walter Hylton, Richard Rolle, and the unknown author of "The Cloud of Unknowing" kindled a fire that was to burn brightly and finally erupt in the Commonwealth some two hundred years later.

The author of "The Cloud of Unknowing" is supposed to have written an English version of the MYSTICAL THEOLOGY of the False Dionysius and to have been a Churchman.[1] Unlike the leaders of the Reformation who wrote in Latin to argue for a vernacular Bible, this author writes in simple English for the benefit of all who could read whether they be scholars or not.

While the book itself is important, it must be viewed as preparing the way for what was to come in the Puritan Reformation. Every revolution needs to feel it is rooted in the past as well as looking toward the future. When the flood of Puritan mystical literature was let loose in England, the names of Dionysius, Julian of Norwich, Walter Hylton, Richard Rolle, Jacob Boehme, and the great host of Fourteenth-Century German mystics were already known to the religious thinkers of the land.

The author of "The Cloud of Unknowing" must be given much of the credit for preparing the ground. It was until the Seventeenth Century, the best work by any English mystic. But more important, the little group of followers that read and cherished this book kept the mystical tradition alive in

---

[1] Sheldon Cheney, *"Men Who Have Walked With God,"* Alfred A. Knopf, New York, 1945, p. 186.

England and provided a nucleous that eventually was swallowed up by the English Boehmists.

"The Cloud of Unknowing" owes much of its popularity to its simplicity and much to its fresh approach to the subject of Christian mysticism.

The simplicity of the path is that man must approach God in three stages. "The first is active works of mercy; here man is below himself; the second is mental prayer or meditation: here man is equal to himself; the third is the contemplation of God: here man is above himself."[2] In one form or another, this has been said many times by other classical mystical writers.

The unique approach in this work is that the author says that God can only be discovered when we venture into the dark cloud of unknowing that exists between God and man.

To the author, as to most mystics, reason appears insufficient. The dark cloud of unknowing cannot be pierced by reason but by divine love, the highest form of knowledge. Reason is not omitted but serves to help man make the initial approach to God. However, it is love that reaches out to receive the love of God which alone can carry us through the dark cloud of unknowing.

Let us now start a spiritual journey with the author. We begin when we understand that we cannot be completely active, nor can we be completely contemplative. The author divides the spiritual life into two categories, the active and the contemplative. He also divides these into two parts. The lower part of the active life "consists in good and honest deeds of mercy,"[3] and the "higher part of the active life and the lower part of the contemplative life lie in good spiritual meditation."[4] Meditation is both active and contemplative. It is active since it consists in "doing something" for God, insofar as conversing with a friend can be called "doing something for him." It is contemplative since in its highest and

---

2 Anonymous, *"The Cloud of Unknowing,"* Harper & Brothers, New York, 1948, pp. 13-15.

3 *Ibid,* p. 14.

4 *Ibid.,* p. 14.

best form, it is not "doing something" but being in His presence. He also calls it "active" since much of the meditation may consist of reflections on the wretchedness of man accompanied by sorrow and repentance.

The higher part of the contemplative life rests "wholly within the darkness of this Cloud of Unknowing with a longing love for God alone and the pure contemplation of Him."[5]

"In the lower part of the active life, a man is outside of himself and beneath himself (he reaches out and stoops down to the physical needs of his fellow Christians with materials quite other than himself.) In the higher part of the active life and the lower part of the contemplative life, a man is within himself and even with himself (looking within he knows the common substance of mankind.) In the higher part of the contemplative life he is above himself and under his God . . . "[6]

As long as he is concerned with himself and his own mental and spiritual processes, he cannot reach this highest step. "He is above himself because his purpose is to go by grace where he cannot go by his own human nature."[7] In this contemplation man is "knit to God in spirit—in oneness of love and harmony of will."[8] This is not union with God but a prelude to it and to some extent, a preparation.

However, before man can go further than this oneness of love, he must cease from the activity of the lower degree for a time. This may seem strange, but the author says something even stranger, that the highest degree of contemplation cannot be reached unless a man cease for a time from meditation.

For we are always in danger that when God would receive us unto Himself, we may fail to respond because we are too busy with our fellowman, or even paradoxically, too busy

---

[5] *Ibid.*, p. 15.

[6] *Ibid.*, p. 15.

[7] *Ibid.*, p. 16.

[8] *Ibid.*, p. 16.

with the affairs of God. Our minds may be so filled with the thoughts about God that we have no room for Him.

But, before we come to this, most of us have to begin at the bottom of the ladder and work so that our minds may be directed from even lesser things than these to the things of the spirit. Indeed we may have to tear our minds away from what is sinful, and trivial, and direct them to consider what is spiritual and vital..

The contemplative apprentice, according to the author, will begin with Lesson, Meditation and Orison; that is, reading, thinking and praying. He leaves these to another unnamed teacher of whom he says, "You can find these three written of in another book by another man in a much better way that I can explain them—therefore, I will not tell you of them here."[9] (It is my opionion that the work is not "Theologia Germanica.")

These, he says, are so tied together that they are in reality one. For thinking cannot take place without reading or hearing coming first. Neither can prayer be had unless there is thinking or meditation first. Not for him is rote prayer or prayer based solely on emotion and involving little or no thought.

In fact, he suggests that the novice, that is, the contemplative apprentice, leave prayer alone until he has learned the meaning of prayer. No boy, he says, should indulge in his former exercises when he is about to learn a game. First, he must learn the purpose of the play, the rules, and then he practices the exercises. "When he enters the game, itself, he fixes his desire on the goal and forgets his former busyness with rules."[10]

Let's look at what he proposes we should do first. We must learn the purpose of the play. What is the end we seek? Is it to do good? Find a heaven? See God? Know God? Be one with God? Fulfill the purpose of our creation?

What are the rules? Must we purge ourselves completely? How much do we do, and how much can we expect from God? Who makes atonement? If we do, how do we atone?

---

9 *Ibid.,* p. 21.
10 *Ibid.,* p. 23.

Lastly, what are the exercises that will strengthen us in our desire to reach out and seize the Pearl of Great Price? Is there any one pattern, or are there many? Does it consist of doing, or of being, or of both? Can we really "do" anything to merit God's Grace, or do we merit God's Grace by becoming? What do we mean by becoming?

All of these questions are answered for us, slowly, painstakingly, and methodically by the author of "The Cloud of Unknowing."

Where do we start? With intent! The author says, "Let there be but a naked intent unto God alone, and not to anything that He has made. See to it that you struggle on against anything except God Himself, so that no other thought dwells in your heart or moves your will but Himself.[11]

"The Cloud of Unknowing" is the first of the great classics to caution against fighting sin. We do not purge ourselves by driving sin out, but by bringing righteousness in. We cannot fill our hearts with righteousness and God by letting our minds dwell upon sin. On the other hand, if we dwell upon righteousness and God, our hearts will soon be too full for anything else but that which comes from on high. God will not forsake us, but as earnestly as we seek Him, He will seek us. The creature that has within him that faculty of comprehending by knowing and the power of comprehending by love, will find that God is ever ready to receive him. Once we contemplate God with our mind and heart, we shall be astonished at the marvelous increase in our desire which God, Himself, implants within us by His Grace.

But first, a man must seek God with all his heart and all his mind, and then shall all the rest be added unto him. The promise is from Jesus, and the author tells us that unless we begin here to fix our intent upon God and His righteousness, we shall not begin at all.

---

[11] *Ibid.,* pp. 23-24.

Chapter IX

Nicolas Herman

Almost no one knows the name of Nicolas Herman, yet millions know him by the name of Brother Lawrence. A native of Lorraine, he served as a soldier in the wars against the Protestants, and then, after a profound religious experience, he became a man servant in the household of one M. Fieubert.[1] Of these years, almost nothing is known.

We know that in 1666 he was in a Carmelite Monastery and was interviewed by M. Beaufort, Grand Vicar to M. de Chalons.[2] Mr. Beaufort recorded four conversations that reveal the spiritual life of the man called Brother Lawrence.

These four conversations, together with fifteen letters and a group of maxims are the entire literary legacy of Brother Lawrence. They are extremely simple, and unless one studies them carefully, it is easy to underestimate their worth. They have served many people for several centuries and the answer lies in the simplicity of Nicolas Herman's approach.

He insists that one thing is needful and that is to direct the soul toward God day by day, hour by hour, and minute by minute. God is by our side, and anyone who is interested in God may converse with Him and experience His presence.

He states to M. Beaufort that he believes "That we should establish ourselves in a sense of God's presence by continually conversing with Him; that it was a shameful thing to quit His conversation to think of trifles and fooleries."[3]

Brother Lawrence makes it seem easy, and most natural. He says, "That in order to form a habit of conversing with God continually and referring all we do to Him, we must at first apply to Him with some diligence; but that after a little

---

[1] Sheldon Cheney, "*Men Who Have Walked With God*," Alfred A. Knopf, New York, 1945, p. 292.

[2] Nicolas Herman, "*The Practice and the Presence of God*," Fleming H. Revell Co., New York, 1895.

[3] *Ibid.*, p. 8.

care, we should find His love inwardly excites us to it without any difficulty."[4]

Like most mystics, Brother Lawrence puts very little faith in the intellect but instead, trusts the loving heart. If we would but return to God some of the love He has for us, our souls would be at peace.

In the second conversation, Brother Lawrence gives a very clear and concise statement of his life's purpose. "I engaged in a religious life only for the love of God, and I have endeavored to act only for Him; whatever becomes of me, whether I be lost or saved, I will always continue to act purely for the love of God. I shall have this good at least, that till death I shall have done all that is in me to love."[5]

To converse with God was the beginning, the middle and the end of life. What the consequences may be or where they would lead did not in the least concern Brother Lawrence. This, as he saw it, was his obligation and his privilege.

The conversations were carried on as Brother Lawrence went about the business of the monastery. He was the cook and God was with him in the kitchen. Except for an occasional trip to purchase wine for the monastery, Brother Lawrence spent the remainder of his days in the monastery kitchen.

He did not seek or even want the special times set aside for prayer. Since his every waking hour was one continuous prayer, he did not think of the set times as different from any other time.

Apparently, he was inclined, at first, to regard the set hours for prayer as interruptions, but soon used them exactly as he had used the hours in the kitchen. Whatever spiritual obligations he had, he observed, but apart from the requirements, his devotional life consisted of practicing the presence of God.

He was quite frank about this in his conversations with M. Beaufort, and he even went so far as to indicate that he

---

4 *Ibid.*, p. 10.

5 *Ibid.*, p. 10.

felt no need of a spiritual director. He did say that he needed a confessor to absolve him, but other than that he consulted nobody, for he relied on the ever present God to direct all his actions.

When we consider the times and realize that much of the Church was engaged in a constant hunt for heretics, it is to the credit of Brother Lawrence's superiors that they did not attempt to silence this independent spirit.

Since neither M. Beaufort nor his superior, the Cardinal de Novailles, have left any personal record concerning their reasons for seeking out Brother Lawrence, we can only guess at their motives. It may be that they had heard of a truly spiritual monk, and they sought to learn what they could concerning him. It may also be that they came in answer to complaints. In the fourth conversation Beaufort includes some material from other sources and makes this ominous statement: "Being questioned by one of his own society (to whom he was obliged to open himself) by what means he had attained such an habitual sense of God, he told him that, since his first coming to the monastery, he had considered God as the end of all his thoughts and desires, as the mark to which they should tend, and in which they should terminate."[6]

Whoever acted as the "inquisitor" felt the need, apparently, of having someone other than himself make a decision concerning this monk. Or it may be simply that having relayed the information, his report attracted attention. That there was some concern about this unusual man and his way of devotion is indicated by the fact that these conversations with Beaufort were not published until 1692, a year after the death of Brother Lawrence.[7]

At times Brother Lawrence came painfully close to expressing strong criticism of monastic life. "Many," he said, "do not advance in the Christian progress because they stick

6 *Ibid.*, p. 28.

7 Sheldon Cheney, *op. cit.*, p. 300.

in penances and particular exercises while they neglect the love of God, which is the end."[8]

Granted that Beaufort could agree with this spirit, such a statement in the hands of an inquisitor could be twisted to imply that the spiritual exercises of the Church have no worth. Yet, the worst that could be said about Brother Lawrence's viewpoint might be that he felt that loving God was sufficient unto itself.

His was not a spirit of controversy, but he was so meek, humble and truly genuine that only the most difficult of persons could misinterpret what he said.

The test and only test that Brother Lawrence would accept was a pragmatic one, "Did this or did that particuar exercise lead one to God?" Any exercise could, if the person using it honestly and fervently sought the presence of God. On the other hand, the same exercise could be used as an escape from the very One whose Name was invoked.

He said, "That our sanctification did not depend upon *changing* our works, but in doing that for God's sake which we commonly do for our own."[9]

The way of Nicholas Herman is deceptively easy. When he says that prayer is nothing else than the sense of the presence of God and that it ought differ from no other time, we are apt to stress the second part and forget the first.

It is apparent that Herman regards the presence of God as an actual presence no less real than the actual presence of one of our fellowmen. In fact, the presence is really an overpowering one. Too often many think of the presence of God as some kind of vague remembrance like feeling the ongoing influence of Lincoln or Washington.

To Herman, God is a constant companion and so absorbing that he might not notice the presence of others, although he never seemed to fail to sense the presence of God.

This sense, he says, comes to those who believe, hope, and love, and to one who perseveres in the three, it comes almost easily. In due time he said that for him "it would be

---

8 Brother Lawrence, *op. cit.*, p. 15.

9 *Ibid.*, p. 16.

as difficult . . . not to think of God as it was at first to accustom myself to it."[10] He recommended this way of life to others by word and by example. Beaufort noted that "His very countenance was edifying, such a sweet and calm devotion appearing in it as could not but affect the beholders."[11]

None of the hustle and bustle of the kitchen seemed to disturb this appearance and the accompanying peace of soul.

---

[10] *Ibid.*, p. 19.

[11] *Ibid.*, p. 19.

Chapter X
Jacob Boehme

One of the criticisms often made against Protestantism is that it never produced any great saints. One recent convert to Catholicism stated, "There must be something lacking with a religion that has never produced a saint, all the great saints are Catholic."

But Protestantism has produced many great saints. In fact, the Evangelical Church gave the world a great saint, in the same century in which it was born.

Jacob Boehme, born in Old Seidenberg of Evangelical parents, received the thorough religious education of a 16th Century Lutheran. The one book that became a companion to Jacob was the Bible, in Luther's translation. Of secular education, he had little beyond the knowledge of reading and writing.

He did, however, receive a good training in the cobbler's trade, which was to earn for him a good living the rest of his life.

During his apprenticeship, he was a zealous, if not a tactful Christian. He attended public worship at the Evangelical Church at Goerlitz with regularity and was outspoken in his attitude toward those who broke the Commandments. It was because of his criticism of several customers who broke the commandment against taking God's name in vain that Jacob was discharged before completing his apprenticeship. His employer said he did not need a missionary.

After that Jacob spent two or three years as an itinerant shoemaker, and we are reminded of Paul's three years in the Arabian desert. For Boehme, those years proved a useful period of training and education. He saw the state of the Church and was disturbed by the cross currents of conflict that divided Lutheran from Lutheran, and Lutheran from Reformed, and Evangelicals from Roman Catholics. Too often the battles were conducted not by pious Churchmen, but by opportunists and political climbers who had no concern for the Church.

Unfortunately for Jacob Boehme, this aversion for argument was to be his cross, for not only was dispute part of the spirit of the times, but Boehme's writings were to stir the Churchmen to anger.

After a severe state of melancholy induced by what he had seen and heard in his travels, he had a profound spiritual experience. But it was some time after that he wrote his first book, "The Aurora," in which he described his experiences. He soon after set up as a master cobbler and married one Katharine Kunshmann. She proved a very able helpmeet and raised a family of six children.

He had many personal experiences with God, most of them taking place while he was at work at his cobbler's bench. We are struck by the similarity to the Catholic Brother Lawrence who practiced the presence of God while working in the kitchen.

He was regular in his duties toward the Lutheran Church at Goerlitz, but had to endure much at the hands of a particularly narrow and bigoted pastor, one Gregorius Richter.

Apparently, Boehme did not feel inclined to share his spiritual experiences with his pastor, and this may have been one of the factors in the breach between them. Boehme kept his own counsel until 1612 when he felt moved to put his religious experiences in writing. The manuscript might never have become public had not one Karl von Endern, a nobleman, discovered it while visiting the cobbler's shop. Von Endern borrowed the manuscript and began to circulate it among friends. Boehme suddenly found that his work was well known among many of the notables.

News of Jacob's fame was not long in reaching his pastor, who apparently did not look with favor upon Jacob's experiences. One Sunday, in the summer of 1613, Pastor Richter delivered a sermon on "False Prophets," a sermon which everyone knew was directed against Jacob Boehme. The charge was one of heresy and blasphemy, and Pastor Richter showed every intention of pushing his charges as far as they would go.

He brought charges before the City Council and requested that they banish Boehme, and at first they consented, but apparently Boehme had enough friends to get the Council to rescind their order.

Though the order was rescinded, Jacob had to pledge to write no further books and to leave the teaching of religion to those who were properly appointed.

For awhile the compromise worked out quite well, except that religious men and women of all ranks of life began to beat a path to the door of the shoemaker of Goerlitz.

Pastor Richter did not entirely honor his promise to cease attacks on Boehme. He may have been irked by the sight of so many notables visiting the cobbler's shop, or perhaps it was a certain narrowness of soul. Richter was neither broad enough of mind, nor sympathetic enough of heart to understand Boehme's attitude toward the Church.

Boehme was one of those who did not regard the Reformation as completed. Though he never considered himself to be in opposition to the Lutheran Church, his frequent attacks on the legalism of some of its servants were sharp, and Richter may have felt, and with some justice it might be said, that he was among those attacked.

Boehme's attacks, if they may be called such, were not intended to provoke controversy. In fact, by temperament, he was unaggressive and of a very humble nature.

Protestantism is fortunate that Richter did choose to attack Boehme again, for these attacks released Boehme from his pledge to cease writing. After much urging by his friends, Boehme again began to write.

His books achieved a simplicity of purpose and aim. Boehme knew God as few men did before him or since. He meant to set down his experiences and provide practical instruction and aids that others might follow in his footsteps. Unfortunately, though Boehme attempted something quite simple in itself, his poor education drove him into using a bizarre vocabulary. As he wished to describe many experiences heretofore not set down on paper, he had need for new words, and these he freely borrowed from the many queer sects that flourished in his time, and gave the words new and orthodox meanings.

Yet, these books of Boehme's constitute the greatest single collection of significant books by a Protestant saint.

His life compares favorably with the greatest of Christian saints, and his influence in his own day extended far and wide. Few religious leaders could have won so great a fame and remained so simple, and humble in their service to God as did Jacob Boehme, Protestant saint of the 16th Century.

Chapter XI

St. John of the Cross
1542-1591

When St. John of the Cross escaped from his prison cell which was ten feet by six, he should have been a broken man, physically and spiritually.

Yet, immediately after his release, he did not seem to want for strength, but gave strength to others. He found haven in a convent which had been founded by St. Theresa, and there he read poems which he had written in prison for the edification and spiritual enrichment of the nuns.

His body was thin, and his voice sounded weak, but those who saw him knew they stood before a tower of strength. Many sought him out during this period to find strength and inspiration.

Yet, this man had lived in a tiny cell for eight months on a diet of bread and water with occasional scraps of salt fish. During this time, he had been beaten almost twice or thrice weekly.

St. John, who had many friends, was in solitary confinement with no means of keeping busy, except toward the last of his imprisonment when he was allowed a little paper and ink. Out of the filth and narrowness of that prison cell came some of the greatest poetry in Spanish. There is nothing to indicate that physical confinement produced any kind of mental confinement. His imagination and mind soared to hithertofore unexplored heights.

Instead of being broken, this man grew and waxed strong; those who saw him did not doubt the source of his strength.

John Yepes was born at Fontibere, Old Castile, in 1542. His father died while he was young, and his upbringing was left to his mother. They lived at Medina where John was sent to the Jesuit College. Here he spent most of his leisure time nursing the patients at the hospital.

At the age of twenty-one, he assumed the Carmelite habit. He was sent to Salamanca to go through a course of theology. Though he gave himself to severe ascetic practices,

64

the Carmelite rule did not satisfy him. He sought about for an order that would make greater demands upon him and thought for awhile of transferring to the Carthusian Order.

However, before he could do this, he met St. Theresa who persuaded him to help her in a reform of the Carmelite Order. St. Theresa was a nun of the Carmelite Order in the Convent of the Incarnation at Avila. She found the Convent far too secular and the discipline too lax. She asked and obtained permission to adopt for herself the stricter and primitive Carmelite rule of life and to found a convent of her Order based upon it.

The convent founded by St. Theresa became the first of the Discalced, or Barefooted Order of Carmelites. This reformed order soon found many adherents among devout women.

The work among the men began in 1568 when St. John took up residence in a house which St. Theresa provided for him at Durvello. Here with Father Antonio, another of St. Theresa's male disciples, he lived until 1569. After Father Antonio left, St. John grew lonely for congenial companionship and encouragement and became quite depressed. The reform had aroused considerable antagonism because of its rapid growth and challenge to the old members of the Order. The Reformers were regarded as runaways from their Order and were even suspected of heresy. St. John's reaction to all this is described in his book, "Noche obscura del Alma." (The Dark Night of the Soul).

This depression left him as he found more and greater responsibilities in the reform movement. In 1570, he transferred to the monastery at Mancera, and also took charge of the new house at Pastrana. From Pastrana, he moved, in 1571, to the new house at Alcala. He did not stay long, for his successor got into difficulties, and St. John had to be recalled to Pastrana to bring back order.

Soon he was called to assist St. Theresa in the reform at Avila. The reformers met considerable opposition, but they had the powerful support of the papal nuncio and the King.

In 1575, the Discalced Carmelites fell under a cloud. The General of the Order sent Father Geronimo Tostado into Spain to press upon the King the necessity of suppressing what he regarded as a schismatic movement. In 1577, John Yepes was imprisoned in Toledo. He received brutal treatment and his health was ruined.

Upon his release, he founded a monastery at Baeza in 1579. The two years at Baeza saw a complete change of fortunes for the Discalced Carmelites. Their work was at long last recognized, and they were established as a separate province, henceforth to run their own affairs without interference from the "unreformed" branch of the Carmelites. John's stay at Baeza was largely spent lecturing in the University there. He seems to have been rather well liked as a teacher, being of a rather humble nature and yet giving much academically and spiritually to his students.

St. John did not care for Baeza since he did not find congenial company. Saint that he was, he still found it difficult to rid himself of a typical Cartilian prejudice against Andalusians. It was therefore with great joy that he accepted his transfer to Granada. As prior of the Monastery of Los Martires, St. John had an opportunity to demonstrate his capabilities as a businessman and an administrator. Contrary to the opinion of his most ardent enthusiasts, St. John was by no means a genius along these practical lines. The most that can be said is that he was able. His genius and his main concern remained in the realm of the spirit. He handled those affairs of this world which came under his stewardship with ability, but he was essentially other worldly.

He attracted men to him as a man of God. As Father Confessor he was sought after; for his experience in the spiritual realm far exceeded that of any other man in his day. This experience is best understood and seen in his poetry. In his poems, notably in "Spiritual Canticle,' he combined lyric genius with great theological insight. He wrote in a day when the Spanish language was coming into full blossom. His prose works edified, but his poetry captivated the soul.

Dr. E. A. Peers, in his splendid biography of St. John, (Spirit of Flame) refers to him as the mystic's mystic. St. John addresses himself exclusively to those who have already renounced the world of temporal affairs as being unreal and who are seeking spiritual reality.

Thus we seek in vain sermons by St. John, for it was not as a preacher but as a pastor that he excelled. Meister Eckhart would instruct the beginner, but St. John was for the advanced student.

The uniqueness of St. John lies in his ability to lead the initiated into heights of spiritual understanding never before expressed so clearly and in so much detail. St. John speaks, without doubt, from experience. We do not have great detail concerning the events during his imprisonment at Toledo, but we have enough to realize that an ordinary man would have come out of prison broken in body and spirit for many months. Yet upon his release, St. John was endowed with unusual spiritual qualities, and during his imprisonment, he wrote some of Spain's greatest poetry. John's cell was evidently occupied by God in a rather unique sense, and in "The Dark Night of the Soul" we have a description of his prison experience that cannot be doubted.

"The Dark Night of the Soul" is an expression given to mystical literature by St. John. It describes an emotional period of depression which is experienced by most Christian mystics. He tends to feel that God has forsaken him and left him to struggle alone in the darkness.

This apparently is a necessary period to temper a man's soul until it is hard enough to endure that which is ahead. After this humbling experience, the spiritual adventurer is more apt to allow God to lead, for he has come to accept his utter dependence upon God.

It is this dependence that marks the writings of St. John. They are simple, easy to follow, but the writer leaves no doubt that he is not the true author. God has used him, hard to be sure, but in order that he might be used in the building of the Kingdom.

He proposes no easy mystical path, but he does propose one that is clear, easy to understand, and well thought out. He is orderly, without being pedantic, he is intellectual, without being cold, and he becomes ecstatic, but his language remains simple. Even though he writes for other mystics, the beginning student, once he has mastered the simple concepts of the mystical way, should consult John Yepes for the clarity and orderliness of his instructions.

Chapter XII
The Mystical Elements in English Puritanism

The Puritan Movement had many roots and owes a debt to many sources. In its earliest beginnings, it was an evangelical movement which owed much to the translation of the Scriptures into the English tongue.

Since the time of John Wycliffe, there was always a small nucleus of people desirous of ecclesiastical change. The Lollard's, as his followers were called, persisted in a small way until they were absorbed into the Puritan movement.

It was undoubtedly Lollard merchants who, almost one hundred years later, helped finance the work of William Tyndale in his translation and publication of the New Testament into English.

While the Continental reformation had its influence, Protestantism in England had indigenous roots. This indigenous Protestantism sought out Geneva in an effort to discover how they might better carry out what they had already determined to do. They would effect an Evangelical reform of the English Church after the pattern of the New Testament.

Calvin's experiment made a profound impression upon many and was found to the liking of English Protestantism in general. During the English Reformation, there were men who thought of themselves as Calvinists, and Lutherans, but their debt to these sources was far smaller than even they, themselves, were aware.

When Elizabeth ascended the throne of England, the Protestants expected that the long awaited reformation would be put into effect. Haller said, "The Puritan movement may be said to have sprung out of the shock of that disappointment."[1]

That disappointment not only caused moderate reformers to become radical reformers, but drove many into temporary

---

[1] Haller, "*The Rise of Puritanism*," p. 8.

exile to Geneva. Here they had opportunity to study, to borrow trenchant arguments from the Calvinists, and issue the Geneva Bible.

Geneva at once became a model Utopia and kept alive the hope that the Church could be patterned according to the Holy Scriptures. The simple service and the preaching of salvation by faith were shared in common by all English Puritans. The form of Church government in Calvin's Geneva became the model for Puritan Presbyterians.

All of this is not to say that the Puritan movement was Calvinist, for the Scriptures continued to be their source, and the Puritan was primarily a student of the Scripture. Theologically, the Puritan owed more to Paul and to Augustine than to Calvin.

As the movement progressed, the Puritans, in spite of difficulties, found ample opportunity to put their ideas into practice.

Out of Cambridge, hundreds of preachers came imbued with Puritan ideas. While they filled the pulpits of the Established Church, their style of preaching, their theology, their attitude towards liturgy and vestments, all marked them as a people apart.

In 1626, William Gouge and Richard Sibbes started a society to raise funds to establish an endowment to maintain Puritan preachers in various pulpits within the Established Church.

For the moderate Puritan, there could be only one fault with the system, and that would be that there were not enough Puritan pulpits and that conformity along with the Puritan pattern was not everywhere immediately established.

Those anxious to secure the Presbyterian system after the Geneva pattern, were at this date (1626) not so numerous, but for them, Utopia had to wait until the Commonwealth.

The Independents had a somewhat easier time than the Presbyterians since single congregations could be established sub rosa fairly simply and aroused less antagonism than the larger unit such as a presbytery.

How many such independent congregations sprung up between 1600 and 1640 is difficult to ascertain, but anyone willing to risk possible, though by no means certain, imprisonment and fine would have no difficulty in finding one in many parts of the country.

All of this religious activity, legal, semi-legal and illegal, was part of a pattern to put into practice the Puritan ideal of the New Testament Church.

At first, each group, according to their own interpretation, was satisfied with outward conformity, at least in the externals, to the New Testament Church.

In the first few decades of the Puritan movement, the average Puritan thought he would be satisfied with a cleansing of the House of God. He would remove the Roman Catholic theological accretions, such as the doctrine of transubstantiation, the episcopal system, and what he regarded as superstitious, liturgical practices. In its place, he would put the plainest type of service in which the sermon held the central place and a Church organized with only such officers as were mentioned in the New Testament. In addition, it was imperative to restore to the clergy and to the laity the morality demanded of them by Christ.

Yet, for all his seemingly preoccupation with externals, such as whether it was right to use the surplice or not, the Puritan was neither shallow nor superficial. The Church must be patterned not only after the external forms of the New Testament Church; it must be a New Testament Church.

This demand for the piety and faith of the New Testament Church soon took one of two forms. Men like Richard Sibbes began to insist upon a spiritual interpretation of Scripture. By this, they referred to the place of the Holy Spirit in the life of the Church.

Since their churches were beginning to be patterned after the New Testament Church, they expected and sought to experience the same sense of the immediacy of the Holy Spirit within their churches, as they felt was experienced in the Apostolic Church.

Others sought this immediate experience with the second Person of the Holy Trinity, Christ Jesus, and among them were such men as Francis Rous and Walter Craddock, who were classical mystics.

The Spirit-mystics were by far the most numerous and influential. They included such men as John Saltmarsh,

70

William Dell, William Erbery, and Thomas Collier. Their popularity was in part due to the fact that many of those who could not be described as mystics shared with these men the same interest in the Holy Spirit, and the doctrines relating to Him. The fundamental doctrine was quite simple; it was stated that not only was the Spirit necessary for the writing of the Scriptures, but also it was necessary for its proper reading and understanding.

Lewis Bayly's, "The Practice of Piety," published in 1615, was extremely popular among all groups of Puritans. In it they were constantly urged to seek out only those preachers who showed a spiritual understanding of the Holy Scriptures.

Hence the mark of the Puritan preacher, for many, was his concern with the Holy Spirit and the doctrines related to this person of the Holy Trinity. But spiritual understanding implied something more. It was an attempt to make every page of Scripture speak to the immediacy of this Person of the Trinity.

The defenders of the Church of England, like Humphrey Sydenham, were especially aware of this mystical interest and were more frightened by it than by the Puritan attempts at "cleansing" the Established Church. Donatism, while abhorrent, at least was understood, and to some extent, the most ardent anti-Donatist must have felt some sympathy and have had some understanding for a group which demanded righteousness upon the part of the servants of the Church.

Sydenham, in a pamphlet in which he views with alarm, significantly enough lumps Brownists and Barrowists with the mystical Family of Love. At least to him, in 1630, they appeared to be part and parcel of the same problem; disturbing the peace of the Church.

He says, "We abhore that age should outdo ours either in Hypocrisy, or Prophaneness, we have our Donatists and Catharists and Anabaptists, as plentifully as they and some besides. *They* had not; the Brownists, the Barrowists, and the Familiest . . ."[2]

---

[2] Sydenham, *"Waters of Morah and Meribah,"* p. 8.

Throughout Puritan literature, and especially the diaries of the men of the time, we find accounts of experimental religion. Not since the 14th Century, when the Friends of God appeared on the Continent, had so many appeared to claim direct, immediate, personal experience with God.

Typical is this statement by Walter Craddock, "I remember in such a country, in such a chamber, in such a place, where God shew'd Himself to me, and I was satisfied; I saw everything vanish before me, and I desired nothing but that . . ."[3]

Craddock is a typical classical mystic insisting that "It is a peculiar privilege of a Saint and ever was and ever will be to see God, to see the King of Glory, the Lord of Hosts."[4] This sight of God, however, is imperfect and transitory and cannot be demonstrated. A typical Puritan, Craddock is a thorough Evangelical contending that the sight of God must come by the Word, a typical classical mystic in that he contends the sight of God is only in Christ, and then, variously, that is, not in the same manner to all.

With Craddock there are never the extremes of moral freedom, since the evidence that a man has seen God is demonstrated by his purity of heart, and a love for the brethren.

The Church to Craddock is something more than an expedient arrangement of God's people. It even goes beyond attempting to copy the mere framework of the New Testament Church. The Church relationship is a direct outcropping of the immediate and personal apprehension of God.

Craddock puts it this way, "When I have seen God and have had fellowship with God and his son, Jesus Christ, I have a spiritual fellowship with all that have seen God with me, that is, the ground of fellowship and communion I have with others is in that they have seen God as well as I; and the impression of God is clear on their spirits and manifested in their lives."[5]

---

[3] Walter Craddock, *"Gospel Holiness,"* pp. 36 f.

[4] *Ibid.,* p. 3.

[5] *Ibid.,* p. 59.

All of this is not to say that the Puritan movement consisted entirely of mystics or even that it was mystical in its essential nature. It was a complex movement which included many elements. The majority of Puritans were undoubtedly Evangelicals in their piety. The Scriptures were the Font of Truth and from them their theology, their polity, and their piety flowed forth. It is true that they approached the Scriptures often through Calvin's eyes, but more often through Augustine's eyes. Along with St. Paul, these two men constituted the major theological influence upon the Puritan movement.

Attempts have been made to describe Puritanism as Covenant Theology, but this is oversimplification. For Puritanism is Covenant Theology, just as it is Calvinism, mysticism, rationalism, or as it may be defined by some as consisting primarily of God's Law, or finally as an Evangelical movement. All of these factors are woven together, and the dominant force depends upon the time, place, and person.

The mystical elements made their appearance early, sometime before 1615.[6] Roughly speaking, in its earliest appearance, it was mainly concerned with the question of extra-Scriptural revelation. In the first part of the 17th Century, most Puritans, including such men as Sibbes, would have answered that the Holy Spirit does not speak apart from the Scriptures. But as time progressed, bolder spirits sought the Light which John Robinson predicted might "yet break forth from His Blessed Word of Truth."

In the middle period from 1630-1660, there appeared numerous classical and spirit-mystics with varying attitudes on this question. Later, men like Morgan Llowd came close to anticipating the Quakers and their particular form of Spirit-mysticism. From 1640 on, both the Quakers and the Spirit-mystics appeared in numbers which alarmed the more moderate Puritans.

It must be pointed out that while the Spirit-mystics had

---

6 The date of the publication of Lewis Bayly's, "*The Practice of Pietie*," but Richard Sibbes had been preaching since 1609 at St. John's College. His sermons led many to the Puritan preoccupation with the doctrine of the Holy Spirit.

much in common with the Quakers, the Puritans differed from both the Quaker and the Spirit-mystics in at least four respects.[7]

1. First, the Puritan was confident that the Holy Spirit did not exclude Reason.

2. Second, the Puritan feared that the Quaker had an inclination to judge Scripture by the Spirit, and repudiate the Evangelical conviction that what was not of Scripture was not, therefore, of Divine origin.

3. Thirdly, many Puritans felt that the spiritual revelation of the Scriptures was an extraordinary dispensation, and while such an extraordinary dispensation might be repeating itself, it was doubted whether such Spirit guidance was to be accepted as an everyday rule.

4. Fourthly, the Quakers taught that the Holy Spirit was present in all men, whether they be imperfect or not. This conflicted with the Puritan idea of election and the idea that the Holy Spirit was limited to those who were among the redeemed.

The Puritan Movement, which existed from 1570-1680, produced a surprising number of distinctly mystical works and at least one denomination which to the present day remains somewhat mystical in its piety. Such books as Rous', "The Mystical Marriage," and Walter Craddock's, "On Gospel Holiness" are as fine descriptions of the mystics' experiences and piety as are to be found in Church literature. The Quaker movement has shown a remarkable ability to survive with its essential ideas still basically unaltered after 300 years.

It is even possible that Congregationalism owes a debt to the mystical elements in English Puritanism. That is not to say that Browne and Barrow were mystics, for essentially they were Evangelicals seeking to revive the pattern of the New Testament Church. But their Evangelical pattern was a vehicle for the faith of men like Craddock, and it was to

---

[7] Geoffrey F. Nuttall, *"The Holy Spirit in Puritan Faith and Experience,"* pp. 155-156.

these men that Congregational polity appealed. Without their support, and their particular piety, the Brownist Congregations, without exception, might have gone the way of the Amsterdam group and splintered into nothingness for the lack of a unifying experience with God to bind them together.

However, except for Craddock's statements and Humphrey Sydenham's criticism, there is little to support this hypothesis, except that mysticism reached its highest peak during the Commonwealth, precisely when Congregationalism emerged from its feeble infancy to become a force which not only had strength, but commanded the respect of thinking Englishmen.

Behind such men as Goodwin, Nye, Bridge, Burroughs, and Simpson at the Westminster Assembly, was not the memory of Browne and Barrow but the more recent experience of the Congregational Chaplains in the Army of the Commonwealth and of Congregations during the Commonwealth that managed to function with a degree of order.

The distinguishing mark that they sought in their preaching was their concern for spiritual understanding. Men like John Owen preached sermon after sermon on the Holy Spirit, and Walter Craddock would have the Church not simply composed of those who believed, but only those who had seen God.

Whether this was true of most of the Congregationalists or of most of their churches, is a task for further research, but it was undoubtedly true of many of the men whose names have come down to us, and it was thought to be true of their churches by Humphrey Sydenham.

Chapter XIII
William Blake

William Blake was one of the few mystics that seemed born to be a dissenter. His father, James Blake, was an attendant at Moravian services in 18th Century England. In addition, he read Swedenborg's books, and his son was apparently acquainted with the ideas of both groups.

It is easy to see where Blake got many of the subjects for his great paintings and for his poems. Like many in the Moravian Church, he was acquainted with Jacob Boehme's works. The elder Blake was both pleased and cautious about his child's early "visions." He urged William to be critical and even doubt, if necessary, some of his earlier "visions."

Later, he became convinced that he did not have an ordinary child, though we are today inclined to regard the child as ordinary, but his early training as extra-ordinary. He endeavored to provide William with an education so that he could give free reign to his imagination. William indicated he would be happy in the arts and was consequently entered as a student at Pars' Drawing School in the Strand.[1]

After he finished his school, he was apprenticed for a 17-year term to James Basire, a good, but not great engraver.[2] Blake was a good student, and in addition to learning his engraving trade, he began to write poetry.

At 24, he married Catherine Boucher, who was his life-long partner and ideally suited as his wife. She had implicit faith in everything he did and was quite willing to assume the life of poverty that a visionary artist-poet would give her.

For the first few years of their marriage, Blake continued to work as an engraver and made poetry and art his spare-time activities. However, he was not content to so prostitute himself, and he increasingly took the impractical road and gave more time to poetry and non-commercial art.

---

[1] Sheldon Cheney, "Men Who Have Walked With God," p. 317.
[2] Ibid., p. 318.

Blake is unique among the mystics in being highly critical of both the Government and the Established Church. Even the sect of his father did not suit him as he found too much legalism and literalism for his taste in much of Swedenborg's writings.

In his two booklets, "There is No Natural Religion," and "All Religions Are One," he warns against conceiving life as limited to sense perceptions.[3] However, his basic doctrines are best set forth in verse, and in "The Marriage of Heaven and Hell," we have a clear insight into the beliefs of Blake.

Here is, for the first time, a mystic turned publisher. Blake felt he had a mission and a prophecy which needed to be revealed. He was at war with the world, and its twin demons, materialism and lack of vision.

Blake has been pictured as an impractical businessman, but the criticism is based not on what Blake could do and frequently did, but what he chose to do. Blake frequently labored to publish poems and engravings that brought little return financially. To make ends meet, he had to turn to more commercial engraving. That he could make a living and find time to turn out art and poetry of great value, speaks of financial competence of the first order. Occasionally, he found a patron, such as Thomas Butts, who recognized his genius and made it possible for him to work some time doing those things which Blake felt were of primary worth.

Occasionally, these patrons presented problems, as when William Hayley decided Blake's mysticism stood in his way of making money. Hayley would reform the mystic and make him a hard-minded businessman who would produce salable works.

However, Blake had no difficulty rejecting the idea completely and continued on his own impractical, yet nevertheless "successful" path. He didn't amass a fortune, but he did succeed in publishing a vast amount of material which would never have been produced if others would have had to publish it. He ran a one-man "vanity press" and produced literature

---

3 *Ibid.*, p. 329.

and art that publishers later were anxious to publish and did so with profit to themselves.

Blake's mysticism reflects his background and his wide reading. In the fourth book, "Jerusalem," he indicates the following steps or stages of spiritual progress.

Step one is the awakening.

Step two is the passing through affliction, or a "Dark Night of the Soul." It is brought about by the realization that one lives not in a real world, but in an illusion of materialism.

Step three is the realization that the world and "unillumined" religion are enemies to spiritual growth. Here, the true mystics practice forgiveness on a vast scale.

Step four, the pilgrim arrives at the realization that part of every man is divine and is illumined by visions which bring him into fellowship with Christ and man.

From here, every other step is inevitable and almost imperceptible. Oneness comes, indeed it must come that the prophecy be fulfilled: "God becomes as we are, that we may be as He is."[4]

---

[4] *Ibid.*, p. 475.

Chapter XIV

Johann G. Hamann
1730-1788

Johann Georg Hamann was born in Konigsberg on August 27, 1730. He was educated in private schools and matriculated to the University at the age of 16. He studied under Martin Knutzen as did his lifelong friend, Emmanuel Kant. Knutzen taught philosophy and mathematics and was a curious combination of pietist and rationalist.

Hamann was not particularly interested in his studies, and though he switched early from theology to law, he left in November, 1752, without taking a degree.[1]

Upon leaving the University, he took a position as house tutor with a Baltic noble family near Papendorf. This post lasted but a short while since Hamann was too demanding a tutor for this family. His second post was happier, and Hamann stayed for several years with a pleasant and well-ordered household at Grunhof. In 1756, he was persuaded by a well-to-do friend, J. C. Berens, to enter his employ as a combination 18th Century lobbyist and business representative.

While in England on business for Berens, Hamann had a religious experience that was to change his entire mode of life. Upon his return to Riga, he allowed Christoph Berens to skim the pages of some notes he had written entitled, "Thoughts About My Life."[2] Berens read them with loathing, for Hamann had turned his back upon the ultimate authority of reason. Berens was more than an employer, for the relationship had grown out of his respect for the intellectual capacity and accomplishments of Hamann. He tried to persuade Hamann of the foolishness of his new position and even managed to get Kant to speak to Hamann and urge him to take a different course.

Hamann was determined to break with the past and to

---

[1] Ronald G. Smith, "*J. G. Hamann,*" Harper & Brothers, New York, 1960, p. 28.

[2] *Smith,* p. 50.

live according to his new found ideas. From 1759 until 1763, he continued to live in his father's house, caring for his aged parents. In 1762, he entered into a common law marriage with Anna Regina Schumacker who became his lifelong partner and companion. During this period, he read widely and wrote many of his important papers and letters. After his father's death, Hamann secured a job in the Customs office, which paid him a modest salary, and continued to devote much of his time to writing and to editing "Kanter's Journal, the Konigbergshe Gelehrte und Politische Zeitungen." He held the Customs post until a year before his death, meanwhile devoting the greater part of his time to his first love, reading and writing.

That Johann Georg Hamann was liked and respected by so many of the leading intellectuals of his day, speaks not only for their tolerance but for the remarkable personality of the man. His thought and life ran against their current. The rationalism of Bacon, Locke, Hume, with their sense-bound empirical philosophy, was accepted by all but the pietist and orthodox thinkers of the day. Since Hamann was equally at odds with the rationalists and the religious thinkers, he was a voice crying in the wilderness.

In the "Age of Reason," Hamann's presupposition for truth was faith. In a letter to Kant, Hamann wrote, "Reason is not given to you in order that you may become wise, but that you may know your folly and ignorance."[3]

Hamann insists that reason cannot lead men to truth, since ultimate truth begins where reason ends. To a man like Hume, the Christian religion can only be believed if we can accept the miracles; and since, according to Hume, no reasonable man can accept them, Christianity ceases to be a live option. To Hamann, this is the ultimate folly, for when reason carries a man to a dead end, this is the time for a step into the dark on faith. Faith, through God's continuous revelation will unlock the secrets that exist beyond the finite nature of man's mind.

His theory of history is significant since he respects the

---

[3] *Smith*, p. 50.

purpose of historical inquiry and its methods while insisting that history is also God's unfolding revelation. Here his thinking runs parallel with the English Puritan Movement, which sought in the signs of the times, evidence of God's directions to mankind.

To Hamann, God was evident everywhere, and nothing could exist without God. One of the most widely debated questions of his time was the origin of language. Hamann insisted upon the divine origin of all speech. He could not accept the Aristotelian position that language was established by arbitrary agreement nor the naturalistic theory of Hobbes that it arose out of the social instincts and needs of man. This is not to say that he held the orthodox view of men like Bishop William Warburton, who claimed that language was the result of a direct and miraculous intervention of God.

Hamann's arguments are not those of the orthodox, "Thus speak the Scriptures," nor of the rationalists who could argue from a psychological investigation of language and its history. He is concerned with the nature of man and man's relationship with God. The reality of man's life depends utterly upon God and upon man's response to God's Word to him. Whatever man does or accomplishes, he does because God permits him to do it. Therefore, whatever man's achievements, the credit belongs not to him but to his Maker. Man has to be taught everything.

Hamann's views were not widely accepted, but they were widely read and widely known. He is a solitary figure of his century who formed a link between the German mystics, Eckhart, Boehme, Tauler, and Suso, with the anti-rationalist romantic thinkers like Herder, Schelling, Kirkegaard, and Bergson. In many ways, he was the first of the existentialists, for without any doubt, he was deeply admired by Herder and Goethe, and through these men, many of his ideas filtered.

He taught in no school, and as a tutor, he had few pupils. Yet, his ideas of the origin of truth are at the very root of all education. Hamann would not understand American secular education since, for him, all truth was God given and was acquired for the purpose of existing in this world in harmony with God. Man learned because God intended that he should learn. Only through learning could man know the Will of

God. This Will was to be found in history, philology, philosophy, in fact, everywhere. We study science, mathematics, history, and language, and while all learning proceeds only with the help of God, all learning has for its ultimate lesson knowledge of God's eternal and immediate will. God's will is not hidden but written into the fabric of life. And, as many men study the Scriptures in order to know the Will of God, Hamann studies the world about him.

Hamann lived in an age hostile to mysticism. It was the Age of Enlightenment when reason was to usher in a new and better world. Many of Hamann's close friends and associates were among the leading thinkers of the movement and found themselves unable to understand Hamann's position. To Emmanual Kant, Hamann's awakening was a burial, and while they continued to be friends, Kant continued to regard Hamann not only as lost but lost without excuse. To the leaders of the Enlightenment, it seemed impossible for a man of Hamann's intelligence and ability to adopt a position so "anti-intellectual."

The heresy of Hamann was to argue, as he once did, with Kant, that "Reason is not given to you in order that you may become Wise, but that you may know your folly and ignorance; as the Mosaic law was not given to the Jews to make them righteous, but to make their sins more sinful to them."[4]

Unlike many of the leaders of the enlightenment, Hamann goes as far as he is able with reason and then insists that when one arrives at the end of the course, he must go further on faith.

Now, by faith, he means something different than the approach of the traditional churchman. First of all, it begins with Socratic ignorance. Once we admit we know nothing, then we truly become teachable.

Beyond the feeble efforts of reason is intuitive knowledge that comes when one knows and loves God. Knowledge is like holiness . . . He does not advocate any particular discipline for achieving it or for seeking God. If Jacob Boehme courts God with an ardour and a directness that, at times, seems

---

4 *Ibid.*, p. 50.

embarrassing, Hamann is so indirect as to seem annoying. He seeks in a gentle, almost nonchalant manner. He works, and lives as if there was nothing else one could do. From his awakening in London we are confronted with a Hamann who is dissatisfied to live according to the rules of the Age of Enlightenment but who apparently embraces no cause, identifies himself with no particular theology, and speaks of his God not as one who must be sought but as One who Is.

Hamann says so little about seeking God; if anything, he tends to oversimplify man's relationship to His creator. Unlike the other mystics, Hamann says almost nothing about the process of finding God, but instead, intermingles his experiences with those of Scripture in such a manner that the casual reader might believe his religion is second hand or vicarious rather than springing from first hand, direct experiences with God.

Chapter XV

Walt Whitman
1819-1892

Almost everyone who knew Whitman remarked on his appearance. In a nation torn by strife, much of it affected Whitman deeply; yet he appeared calm, and at peace with himself. Though he often appeared firm, he never seemed angry or proud. People seemed to enjoy sitting in his presence.

In his poems, especially, "Song of Myself," he sounds to the uninitiated as one who is obsessed with himself. But Whitman, the man, as distinguished from the poet, is painfully aware of his own inadequacies. He never spoke with the intention of impressing anyone but managed to do so in a simple, humble, and unaffected way.

To Whitman, everyone and everything was beautiful. He seemed to have a natural liking for people of every walk of life and of every background.

His poetry never satisfied him, and it is doubtful whether he ever fully realized the tremendous achievement his poems represented.

Much of his poetry is autobiographical. And we have a vivid account of his illumination which came to him when he was 34 or 35 years of age. He says, "I believe in you, my soul, the other I am must not abase itself to you. And you must not be abased to the other." The new man comes but not to destroy the old, even as it cannot be destroyed by the old but to bring the old man fulfillment. What follows is a description of the change wrought by his experience of illumination.

"Swiftly rose and spread around me the peace and knowledge that pass all the argument of the earth. And I know that the hand of God is the promise of my own, and that all the men ever born are also my brothers, and the women, my sisters and lovers, and that a kelson[1] of the creation is love."[2]

What takes place is not of his own doing but grows out of every man's relationship to God.

"And I know that the hand of God is the elder hand of my own, and I know that the spirit of God is the eldest brother of my own."[3]

From this moment on, Walt Whitman became a man apart. According to Dr. Robert Bucke, who studied him closely, Whitman showed the following characteristics which are evident in all of the great mystics:

a. The subjective light appeared strongly to Whitman.

b. The moral elevation and

c. Intellectual illumination were extreme, and in his case stand out very clearly, since we know the man so well, both before and after the oncoming of the Cosmic Sense.

d. In no other man who ever lived was the sense of eternal life so absolute.

e. Fear of death was absent. Neither in health nor in sickness did he show any sign of it, and there is every reason to believe he did not feel it.

f. He had no sense of sin. This must not be understood as meaning that he felt himself to be perfect. Whitman realized his own greatness as clearly and fully as did any of his admirers. He also realized how immeasurably he was below the ideal which he constantly set up before himself.

g. The change of the self-conscious man into the Cosmic Conscious was instantaneous—occurring at a certain hour of a certain day.

---

[1] Kelson or keelson is a strengthening structure in a ship above the keel and fixed to it.

[2] Walt Whitman, *"Leaves of Grass,"* Penguin Books, New York, 1944, p. 26.

[3] *Ibid.*, p. 26.

h. It occurred at the characteristic age and at the characteristic time of the year.

i. The altered appearance of the man while in the Cosmic Conscious state was seen and noted."[4]

Regarding the latter, Bucke fortunately records one testimony regarding this phenomena in Whitman. Miss Helen Price, a friend of Dr. Bucke, writes these lines:

One evening in 1866, while Walt Whitman was stopping with us in New York, the tea bell had been rung ten minutes or more when he came down from his room, and we all gathered around the table. I remarked him as he entered the room; there seemed to be a peculiar brightness and elation about him, and almost irrepressible joyousness, which shone from his face and seemed to pervade his whole body. It was the more noticeable as his ordinary mood was one of quiet, yet cheerful serenity. I knew he had been working at a new edition of his book, and I hoped if he had an opportunity, he would say something to let us into the secret of his mysterious joy. Unfortunately, most of those at the table were occupied with some subject of conversation; at every pause I waited eagerly for him to speak; but no, someone else would begin again, until I grew almost wild with impatience and vexation. He appeared to listen, and would even laugh at some of the remarks that were made, yet he did not utter a single word during the meal; and his face still wore that singular brightness and delight, as though he had partaken of some divine elixir. His expression was so remarkable that I might have doubted my own observation had it not been noticed by another as well as myself."[5]

The Whitman story is worth a lot of study and research, and I hope it will be down before much of the first hand and personal testimony is lost. Here is a man who lived in a secular society, who was recognized as being a good man and

[4] Richard M. Bucke, "Cosmic Consciousness," E. P. Dutton and Company, Inc., New York, 1946, p. 237.

[5] Ibid., p. 236.

one of great spiritual stature, but the source of his strength was little known. Since Whitman, like Jesus, spent much of his time with people not particularly religious, and since even the elementary understanding of religion was not theirs, they lived in almost total ignorance of the man they thought they knew so well.

Jesus, even when he associated with irreligious people, did not find them religiously illiterate. Hence, we learn as much about Jesus from his secular friends as we do from his religious intimates. Even his enemies have much to tell us about Him. It may well be that much about Whitman will be lost to us since those who knew him best were often incapable of comprehending what they saw and heard.

Chapter XVI
Kahlil Gibran
1883-1931

Kahlil Gibran was once asked, "What is a mystic?" And he replied, "Nothing very secret nor formidable—just someone who has drawn aside one more veil."[1]

He also claimed that he saw and spoke to Jesus on three separate occasions. If this is so, we have then, at least, two pictures of Jesus that have been drawn by someone who has seen Him.

According to his wife, Gibran had several mystical experiences which he described to her, but which, because she promised never to speak of them, she refuses to enlighten us concerning them.

It is unfortunate that these things were revealed to no one but Barbara Young, for she is a poor interpreter of Gibran and his religious faith and experience.

We are not, however, without some tremendous literature, nor are the drawings without their message. First and foremost is "The Prophet," a work condemned by many of the critics of literature but loved by the people.

I value it for some of the deeper insights that it has given us concerning the nature of evil, of man, and of the laws of compensation.

Gibran is presented as an unorthodox son of the Maronite Church, but such is not the case. Of all the mystics, Gibran seems most at home with his church. This is not to say he was in complete agreement with it, nor that the Church regarded him always with favor. He remained a communicant member of the Church of his birth, and his writings and drawings are exactly what one would expect from a mystic springing from this Eastern tradition.

If he did not always give attention to the rituals and observances of the Church, he did give attention to the Jesus of that Church. He views the incarnation as the "first Word

---

[1] Barbara Young, "This Man From Lebanon," p. 95.

of God uttered unto man,"[2] and his entire philosophy and life is Christo-centric.

Like all mystics, he knows great ecstasy, especially after those moments when he has been in the presence of Jesus, but he has also known the dark night of the soul. Once he felt that he was Judas, and for a short time was broken, bent and frightened by the awfulness of the sin that he bore upon his shoulders. For he believed in the essential unity of all mankind. To him, it was impossible to separate the good from the evil, and as long as one of us sinned, we all shared his guilt equally.

To my mind, the chapter on Crime and Punishment in "The Prophet" is one of the great contributions of Gibran. This is mystical insight and vision at its best.

Any wrong to others is wrong to yourself, for it has the effect of keeping you separate from God.

However, sin leaves your "God-self undefiled." Gibran thinks of man as having two natures, God-self and man, or more precisely put, "a shapeless pigmy in the mist."[3]

This second nature, "the shapeless pigmy," knows evil and knows of its punishment. "The holy and the righteous cannot rise beyond the highest which is in each one of you," (nor can) "the wicked and the weak . . . fall lower than the lowest which is in you also."[4]

No evil is committed in this world that does not have the silent consent of all. Even "The murdered is not unaccountable for his own murder."[5]

In fact, the "guilty is often times the victim of the injured."[6] We are like black and white threads woven together, and when the black thread breaks, the weaver shall not only examine both but also the loom.

---

2 Kahlil Gibran, *"Jesus, The Son of Man,"* p. 132.

3 Kahlil Gibran, *"The Prophet,"* p .46.

4 *Ibid.,* pp. 45-50.

5 *Ibid.,* pp. 45-50.

6 *Ibid.,* pp. 45-50.

Because if you cannot separate the just from the unjust, you cannot punish. In addition, there are those whose remorse is greater than their misdeeds and those who are thieves in spirit who have not committed any dishonest deeds in the flesh. Remorse comes to all, "Unbidden shall it call in the night, that men may wake and gaze upon themselves."[7] To one who has known remorse, and who suffered to such an extent that he felt he was the re-incarnation of Judas, it seems incredible that men would inflict any additional punishment upon a man besides that which his own remorse had heaped upon him.

Like all mystics, Gibran teaches that our fate is determined in this life. Death holds no fear for him, for

> "Death changes nothing but the masks that cover
>   our faces,
> The woodsman shall be still a woodsman,
>   The ploughman, a ploughman,
> And he who sang his song to the wind shall
>   sing it also to the moving spheres."[8]

Since Kahlil Gibran was a poet and not a theologian or a philosopher, the way to God, ala Gibran, is not distinctly defined. When we are most anxious for him to talk, he sings to us, and when we would have him sing regarding his own mystical erperiences, he chooses to keep silence.

Yet, through it all, there is the familiar fourfold pattern of awakening, purgation, illumination, and union with God.

The one thing distinctive is the purgation process. With Gibran, it consists of accepting the responsibility for every last sin in the world, be it small or great. Purgation can only come when the individual accepts without attempting to justify, explain or evade responsibility for the evil that exists in the world.

The moments of illumination came during the periods when he was most productive or should we say, it was the other way around. He was most productive when he was illuminated.

---

[7] *Ibid.*, p. 49.

[8] Kahlil Gibran, *"The Garden of The Prophet,"* p. 62.

Barbara Young says he did not talk of his experiences often but "when he did he was like a man touched with the Finger of divine fire, and I could no more have doubted than I could doubt my own existence . . . These exalted experiences came during the writing of the book, 'Jesus, The Son of Man.' To have seen him for one hour during the incalculable travail that resulted in the volume, was to know that this man from Lebanon was in truth of a stuff more divinely woven, and of a pattern more godlike than our own. To have seen him thus transfigured before human eyes was to accept the certainty of his calling, the chosen and the beloved of the high gods."[9]

Stripped of Young's verbosity, it is obvious that Gibran was profoundly affected and probably transfigured during these moments. I suspect, he will be evaluated largely by his accomplishments as a poet and an artist.

Here he is without parallel in our time. His work will make its mark not purely on artistic merits, but like Blake before him, his work will continue to intrigue men because of its mystical revelation.

There will be some who believe his head of Christ is a picture of the Master, one painted not as imagined, but as seen. Likewise, if one can accept this as a picture of Christ, it is not difficult to accept "The Prophet" or any of the other books as "the words of Christ." There are those, like Dr. William Norman Guthrie, "who would treat Gibran's writings as 'the word of God,' or at the very least, as 'The Gospel according to Gibran.' "[10]

I would suggest you suspend judgement until you have spent at least ten years with *The Prophet.* You may not accord it such a high place as this, but I am sure you will discover truths unavailable elsewhere.

---

[9] Barbara Young, p. 98.

[10] *Ibid.,* p. 33.

Chapter XVII

Awakening

Every religious fellowship or movement teaches that in one form or another, there must be a moment of truth. This is a time when the individual finds he must make a decision; that he must take a decisive step that will enable him to begin a new life.

The terminology, the methods, and the mode differ widely, but it is assumed that the act is essentially the same. Whether one calls it conversion, rebirth, new life, change, or even awakening, does not really matter, for they are all essentially the same.

Whenever one studies about religion, he becomes enmeshed in words. We are attempting to describe some profound things and are trapped by the fact that some things simply cannot be expressed adequately because of the limitations of language.

What the mystics experienced in their awakening, they preferred not to explain. It couldn't be explained, or, at least, it couldn't be explained in a way that those of us who lacked their experience could understand.

Human beings have simply not learned to communicate those things which are most worthwhile, and which are closest to reality. Consequently, when the mystics have said anything about their awakening, the words and descriptions used have been interpreted by their listeners in terms of the listener's own experience. In one form or another, people are familiar with what is meant by conversion, and, at first glance it seems as if the mystics had undergone this experience commonly called conversion.

Even this term is not understood by everyone in the same way. It means different things depending upon your background and religious experience.

To some, it simply means exchanging one set of beliefs for another or one religious affiliation for another. It may mean that a person was a Roman Catholic, and he became a Baptist or vice versa. It often means a person with no faith becomes a believing Christian.

But generally speaking, this is held to be a superficial use of the word, and most Evangelical groups have attempted to give it a more profound meaning.

The late Samuel Shoemaker, who thought more about this question and wrote more about it than any modern American, has lifted it out of any superficial context and given it some real meaning. To him, conversion is a moment of self surrender to God. It comes "When we want God's way more than our own."[1]

According to Rev. Shoemaker, it involves four things. First, it involves a rejection of sin. It is, as has sometimes been called, a re-orientation. Once we moved in the direction of sin, but now we turn our backs to sin and walk toward God and His righteousness.

Secondly, we begin to provide time in our daily routine for fellowship with God. This should mainly consist of conversations with Him, (prayer) but it will involve devotional reading, Bible Study, etc.

Thirdly, it involves fellowship with other Christians. No man lives this life alone. You are now members of God's family, and like any good family man you need to stay home and live in the family circle.

Fourthly, we must share what we have. A faith that is not shared dies. It has to; first, because if it is real we shall want to share it, and secondly, because we live in a world where many people want to share their pagan faith with us. The drunkard wants all the world to consist of drunkards. Whatever sinful act you may wish to engage in, there is always someone to help you do it. They do it through kind words of advice or under the guise of being helpful. Some of us, however, are not in danger of being led in the wrong paths, but we are ineffectual in leading others the right way. Shoemaker tells of a friend who said, "That while his friends could not make him drunk, he couldn't make them sober."[2]

---

1 Samuel M. Shoemaker, *"How to Become a Christian,"* Harper Brothers, New York, 1953, p. 78.

But the real tragedy is that this stalemate seldom lasts. When two people come to know one another well, they find a common denominator. There is always a lifting up or a pulling down, and if one has been really converted, he will see the effect in the changed lives of those whom he meets.

Now, all of this is fine, and one cannot quarrel with it, but since we are studying the mystics, we must ask ourselves whether this is what they meant when they talked about their awakening. Perhaps conversion is the same; maybe it is absolutely different, or it may be that conversion, as Samuel Shoemaker defines it, is a part, a small part of what the mystics meant by an awakening.

I think when we look at the place where awakening starts and where conversion starts, we will see the essential difference. Conversion grows out of human need. The classic pattern for Christian evangelism has been to make people aware of the fact that they are sinners. A Chinese proverb says, "A person who finds pleasure in sin is a novice to both."

Sooner or later many sinners will grow tired of their life and seek some form of change. Many people are not especially happy with life. They have found little satisfaction in it, they have found that happiness is not constantly with them, and if they have found joys, they have experienced an equal number of sorrows. Many people are drifting, and life seems to have little purpose; and it certainly doesn't add up, for them, to anything meaningful.

As a result, they want change; they are seeking something to which they can dedicate themselves in the hope that they can find a better life. Many conversions are actually acts of desperation. The repentant sinner may literally cast himself upon God full knowing that he desperately needs to be saved from himself. When God becomes the last, rather than the first resort, it is a questionable experience. Further, the real quandry is that the individual has sought God as an answer to his own problems. Thus, the converted soul is the mover, and God is somehow a heavenly assistant.

I sought God and He helped me! The pattern has been

---

2 *Ibid.*, p. 74.

established, and God will be called upon again and again to help. Someday there will come a time when God seems to fail in this role in which He has been cast, and a faith will be shaken and God lost sight of . . . "My God, my God, why hast Thou forsaken me," they will cry, and there is no answer that is not embodied in the question.

It is only when we think of self that we think in terms of being forsaken. The mystics did not come to God with or because of a conviction of sin. God found them! And when He did, they saw their own shortcomings, and they were repelled by their sins.

For the mystic, purgation comes after the awakening. Many of the so-called converted believe they are saved from sin, from the moment of their conversion. The mystic would feel that no one really knows what sin is until he has come face to face with God, and in the Light of God's Glory, has seen his own miserable and wretched condition.

He is awakened not to sin, to his own unhappiness, his own weakness, but he is awakened to God. He discovers God, who while He has been here all the time, has passed unnoticed, unheeded, and unseen in our midst.

To the mystic, it is a fact that no man can become aware of God without being profoundly affected. We talk of God, we even have certain beliefs about God, but for the most part, we are not moved. We are not moved because God does not seem real! We pretend that we believe in Him, probably because it seems illogical or even stupid to do otherwise.

But, if you believed in God—you would obey Him.

If you believed in God—you would worship Him.

If you believed in God—He would be constantly on your mind, on your lips, and on your heart.

Since He is none of these things to the vast majority of so-called believers, we must assume that their belief is something unreal, or at best, so superficial as to hardly constitute a belief at all.

How can you believe in God and believe in your own goodness? For, by comparison, you must be revolted at the sight of yourself. How can you believe in God and continue not only to commit the same sins day after day, week after week, month after month, but all too often, the thought of sin has long since ceased to bother you. We rationalize, we invent new codes of morality, we temporalize, and make excuses for ourselves. Yet, no man can do any of these things and face God.

The awakening is that moment when God seems so real, that all else seems sham, and its temporal and shadowy quality becomes apparent. When God seems more real than anything or anyone else, the soul has been awakened.

We do not know why the handful of mystics were so moved by God, and sometimes we are not sure how, and under what circumstances. But each and everyone had a point in his life that was a turning point. From that time on, these men were literally "God intoxicated." They knew that "He is."

What they knew was that there was only one significant reality, and it was this reality they sought to know. They wished to become as closely related as was possible to the One they knew to be at the center of the universe. For this they were willing to sacrifice everything, strip themselves naked, and forsake everything.

There was no thought of God helping them to do anything. No thought of God giving them anything, and no prayer to be answered except this one, "Bend my will to thine, O Lord, use me as Thou wilt, and make us One, even as Jesus and Thee are One."

It was not that they repented or acted in any way, and that God responded. It was that God had shown Himself to them, and they responded in the only way that they could—to submit themselves to Him and to seek to know Him fully.

Their approaches before the awakening varied. For the most part, they were merely very sensitive souls, who, as they went through this world, saw what was to be seen, and heard what was to be heard. They missed very little as they traveled on life's trail, and hence, they saw and heard God, where others had passed by and had seen and heard nothing.

Some had a different approach. They saw men on every hand who deluded themselves that they had found God. They professed a faith that bore no fruits. They voiced many things with their lips, but they were not moved to act. The gulf between their profession of faith and their living was too great, and the mystics wondered what was wrong.

Consequently, they sought to find God by discovering what He was not. They became agnostics who sought faith. They questioned everything, every belief, every act, and even cynically, concluded that the so-called good acts of men were often cloaks for self-indulgence and pride. When they were finished, they could say that God was something "Other." And while it might be unsatisfactory to you or to me, everything else having been renounced, they were content to place themselves in the hands of a God, Unknown and Unknowable. Their awakening came when they broke loose from all that was not God, and turned to Him in absolute faith and sought Him in a Cloud of Unknowing.

It matters not how we approach Him, because in reality, it is He Who approaches us. He is here. We are like a small child who is engaged in some act which is forbidden. Then, all of a sudden he senses that someone is in the room with him, and, what is more disturbing, he becomes aware of the fact that someone had been there all the time.

At this point, he drops what he had been doing and turns in fright or for assurance, depending on how he regards the parent. So we act upon awakening to the fact of God's presence. If we see Him as He is, we shall drop whatever we are doing, not out of guilt, but because it is trivial, and turn and devote ourselves to Him.

Chapter XVIII

Purgation

Man finds it difficult to accept God's system of justice because it denies to man a separate identity. Man can in no wise separate himself and his actions from those of his fellowman.

Each man suffers for the sins of all mankind. We pay a price for sin since sin is a social rather than a purely personal act. Like Jesus Christ, we make a vicarious atonement for the sins of all mankind.

We rebel at this, and we look upon those who hurt us as intruders upon our world. We direct our anger, our hatred, and our bitterness toward those who do evil toward us and refuse to regard them as our brothers.

Yet, Gibran says we cannot separate the good from the evil, and that none can sin without the silent consent of us all. Further, he says that none can fall lower than the lowest that is in us all, and conversely, none can ascend higher than the highest that is in us all.

But we do not believe this. Those who hurt us, we honestly believe are worse than we, ourselves. This is because we have not examined ourselves closely enough, and we do not recognize the evil that is within us.

"We stumble because those who have gone before removed not the stone for us, and we stumble as a caution for those who follow."

God does not punish. The hurts and the afflictions we feel, we inflict upon one another. There is a law of recompense. The man who steals another man's wife may not suffer remorse nor receive anything evil at the hands of the injured husband. Yet, insofar as he has helped make the world more evil by his act, he has set in motion a chain reaction that will bring pain to all, including himself.

We are constantly hurting one another. When you cheat me, you are not sinning against me, but you are an instrument of life's justice inflicting upon me the punishment I so richly deserve for my own past transgressions.

We can sin only against God—not against our fellowman.

Sin means estrangement from God. When I strike you, it is not you who are wrongly dealt with, but God. I say this because in the past you have turned your back on God. You have done evil to your fellowman, and probably you deserve whatever you receive at my hands.

But for my part, when I strike you, I am unfair to God. He feels the blow also, and He has not done evil. You and I have disobeyed Him even though He has given us life and blessings which we have not and cannot deserve.

Only God is dealt with unjustly by *our* acts; for if *you* are honest with yourself, you will have to admit that you have not paid for all of your sins. Although you have been abused and used despitefully, you have also contributed your share of abuse.

You will atone for sin, yours and your fellowman's. Like Christ, we are crucified for the sins of the world.

This is why He says, "Blessed are they which are persecuted for righteousness' sake: for theirs is the kingdom of heaven. Blessed are ye, when men shall revile you and persecute you, and shall say all manner of evil against you falsely for my sake. Rejoice and be exceeding glad: for great is your reward in heaven: for so persecuted they the prophets which were before you." (Matt. 5:10-13)

Until we make this vicarious atonement, we cannot receive the kingdom of Heaven.

This is a most difficult thing to do. Daily we pray, "Forgive us our debts as we forgive our debtors," but we don't forgive.

How can we forgive when we do not recognize our own involvement in the sins of others? This comes to us only a few times in our life.

It may come to a father who has been badly used by a son. He may come to the point where he can forgive the son, when he, the father, recognizes that the son is, in part, what the father has made him. When this moment of recognition comes, the father understands the oneness of mankind, and he can forgive.

But usually, the connection is not as easy to see. A man can forgive an adulterous wife, for he may recognize the fact that he helped drive her into adultery. It is not as easy to see how he can be blamed for the actions of the man who intruded into this marriage and took what was not his to take. How can the husband feel that he was involved in this stranger's evil lust? More important, how can he regard him as a brother, forgive him, and love him even as God loves His children?

Yet, are not the victim and the offender both sinners before God? All men have sinned and none are perfect. There is only one sin, that is, disobedience to God. Until I am perfect in obedience and one with God, I stand in the judgement. I shall be judged as a sinner and pay the price for my offenses. My self will suffer sometimes by the evil of others and only occasionally through my own direct actions.

Gibran says that the murdered is not unaccountable for his own murder, and that oftentimes the guilty is the victim of the injured.

This world is what we have made it. It is not pretty, and it is often a very unlovely reflection of ourselves.

In this world, we can never find peace. It is a literal hell on earth from which there is no escape until we have found God.

No man can purge himself and make within himself a fit habitation for God until he has borne upon himself the sins of the whole world.

Until he can look upon the murderer and see in him one who would bring to him punishment which he deserves, he cannot purge himself. Until he can see the murderer as a poor soul who is transgressing not against him, but against God, and until he can feel remorse and sorrow in his heart for this murderer, he cannot, himself, be purged.

"Forgive us our debts as we forgive our debtors." We cannot really forgive until we see ourselves involved in the misdeeds of others.

These evil deeds are our punishment, and they are the outcome of forces that we, ourselves, are constantly setting in motion. No man sins in private, but the evil which he does produces a chain reaction that moves and afflicts us all.

It is only the foolish man who says, "I don't see any

harm in what I have done because it didn't hurt anyone else."

I know of no commandment of God that can be broken which would not hurt *everyone* else in the world.

Much of our behaviour is influenced not by God, but by the moral climate we have created around us. This statement, "I can see no harm . . . " can only be made by one whose awareness of God and His influence in his world is almost non-existent. This awareness may be obscured by the fact that his feelings are governed by a climate created by millions of sinners who have felt as he did and who recognized no law not made by human hands.

Whether such a one can forgive, I do not know, but a God who loves him, created him, and sustains him fortunately can and does. I cannot look upon him as a lesser being since I, too, have not accepted God. If he does me harm, it is because he is like a ship out of control. Since we are all pilotless ships, we cannot blame one more than the other, but must equally share the cost when calamity results.

Until we can see this, we shall have no peace. The resentments we hold, cause us much suffering and pain and we cannot obtain release from this pain until we can forgive. But we cannot forgive until we see ourselves in our brother's evil acts. Until we can identify with the murderer, the adulterer and the thief, and are willing to atone for his misdeeds, we can in no wise purge ourselves and become a fit habitation for the Most High.

Until such time, Jesus tells us, "Judge not that ye be not judged. For with what measure ye mete, it shall be measured to you again. And why beholdest thou the mote that is in thy brother's eye, but considerest not the beam that is in thine own eye? Or how wilt thou say to thy brother, Let me pull out the mote out of thine eye; and behold, a beam is in thine own eye? Thou hypocrite, first cast out the beam out of thine own eye; and then shalt thou see clearly to cast out the mote out of thy brother's eye." (Matt. 7:1-5)

101

Chapter XIX

Illumination

Jacob Boehme's greatest work, "The Way to Christ," consists of a series of tracts designed to help the sincere seeker of God.

It consists of suggestions, prayers, and a series of dialogues. It is in the dialogues that Boehme reveals the most about himself and his ideas. I suspect he adopted this form of writing to protect himself from the criticism of the more orthodox.

As I reread the pages of this book, I was struck with the fact that except in the dialogues, he says little that others have not said before him.

But consider the nature of the following dialogue with Sophia:

> When Christ that Cornerstone within the tarnished human image moves Himself in man's heart by means of his heartfelt conversion and repentance, then through this movement of Christ's Spirit within the tarnished image, the Virgin Sophia appears before the Soul in her virgin's finery. At this the soul in its impurity is so frightened that all its sins are awakened within it so that it falls back again into its unworthiness, being ashamed of its lovely suitor. Introspectively, it begins to castigate itself as altogether unworthy to receive such a treasure. Those who are of us, and who have tasted this heavenly treasure, understand this; others not. But the noble Sophia approaches the Soul's being and kisses it affectionately, tincturing the Soul's dark fire with her Love rays and penetrating through the Soul with her Love kisses. Then, triumphantly, the Soul leaps in its body for great joy, and with the vitality of this Virgin Love, praises the great God—the Might of the noble Sophia.

When this happens, above described, then the Soul rejoices in her Love, and says:

> 46. *Soul:* O mighty God! Now may my praise, thanksgiving, strength, honour and glory be unto Thee in Thy Might and Sweetness, that Thou has released me from the Instigator of anguish! O Thou fair Love! My heart embraces Thee! Where hast Thou been so long? I thought that I was in hell, in God's

wrath! O most charming Love, remain with me! Be Thou my joy and recreation! Lead me in the paths of righteousness! I yield myself unto Thy Love! Before Thee I am dark! Enlighten me! O lofty Love! Just give my sweet Pearl to me! Just place it within me! . . .

47. *Then the Virgin Sophia says to the Soul:* My dear Bridegroom, my strength and might! You are always welcome! Why have you forgotten me so long that I, in grief, was forced to stand before your door and knock? Didn't I always call you, entreat you? But you turned your face away from me, and your ears had forsaken my domain.[1]

Note two things about this dialogue. First, the traditional role of the bride and the bridegroom are reversed. According to Scripture, Christ comes as the Bridegroom to claim his Bride, the Church, and this role Boehme does not change; in relation to Sophia, the seeker is the Bridegroom, but even here there is a peculiar change of roles. The second fact to note is that the Bride seeks the Bridegroom much more aggressively than he seeks her. She, that is Sophia, stands at the door knocking and pleading. There is nothing gentle about her entreaties; she is a wanton, speaking with a passion that would bring blushes to the most sophisticated.

The way to Christ is the way of the suitor. The Heavenly Wisdom, Sophia, seeks a Bridegroom, and consequently, she must be courted.

One simply cannot accept Sophia's love which she offers so freely since, as she states in the dialogue, "You (have) accepted the Devil as your lover, and he (has) defiled you and built up his robber's castle of vanity within you and inclined you away from (Sophia's) Love."[2]

Consequently, the first step is to cast out the unworthy love and prepare for a new, greater and worthy Love, the Heavenly Wisdom, Sophia. She then will come and complete the task of cleansing, and together you will work the purposes which God has intended for you.

Sophia will bring the illumination that will awaken

---

[1] Jacob Boehme, *"The Way to Christ,"* pp. 33-34.

[2] *Ibid.,* p. 34.

a thirst, and a desire for God, Himself. Since we can never fully know God, we must be content to know God's Wisdom. This we can know, and, in fact, enter into an erotic relationship with Her. If one doubts this, read the prayers that Boehme offers to Sophia. One wonders what Mrs. Boehme thought of all this.

Probably she was content to possess what she could of this strange man who was never more than partially in this world.

Sophia brought the heavenly *Tinctur* which transforms the soul of man so that it is no longer conformed to this world. It is difficult to understand whether Boehme felt that the Tinctur which Sophia brought wrought a partial or a complete transformation, though this word appears in his works hundreds of times.

His use of the word in his earlier works is more frequent and seems to be used in connection with almost every illumination, or experience of Christ or Sophia. In his later works, including "The Way to Christ," it is used less frequently and seems to imply a complete and eternal transformation.

With Jacob Boehme there is not the order, the heavenly ladder, that is so common to all the other Western Mystics. While in general he seems to follow the classic path, its progression is less fixed and the so-called "stages" seem to blend into each other. Thus, the process of repentance with Boehme is a never-ending process, and the illuminated man still wrestles with Satan, and the sinner seeks fervently the Virgin Sophia and may even receive illumination.

Illumination in the Boehmist scheme of things is not the result of purgation, but frequently the road to purgation; for the Heavenly Sophia seeks to aid man in his search for God, and this involves helping him to escape Satan, her rival for his love.

Let us now paraphrase the Boehmist Way.

The essence of all true religion is that we love God because He first loved us.

In each of us there is something that responds to love. Once we comprehend the breadth, depth, and height of God's love for us, we are overwhelmed. In our creation, preservation and all the blessings of this life are a great expression of His love for us.

To return this great love becomes at once the object and the end of life. For to this end are we created that we may live in all eternity in fellowship and love with God.

Deep down we crave to love God but are forever torn between the temptations of sentimentality and neglect. Even Scriptures tell us that this love is a most difficult task. We are asked, "How can we love God whom we have never seen when we do not love our neighbor whom we have seen?"

This is man's perennial problem, "How can he love Him whom he has not seen?" Since he cannot, according to Boehme, he can at least love God's Wisdom. Sophia he can see, feel, touch, and taste, if he is at least willing to turn out the harlot, the Devil, and bid Her come in that they may dwell together.

Boehme, like Eckhart, did not accept the Platonist theory that the Idea of God represented the Godhead. The Godhead was too remote, too vast a concept for man's finite mind. Consequently, according to Boehme, God was unknowable, dwelling in the *Ungrund,* the eternity beyond nature and creature.

And so man seeks the Heavenly Wisdom, Sophia, by being attentive to her and courting her. It is not unlike a man's love for his wife. If he truly loves her, he is attentive to her, he does things for her, remembers her on important occasions, brings her gifts, treats her with respect, and in a hundred ways shows that he is interested. A man who loves Sophia is attentive to her, he prays, he tries to live a righteous life, he is reverent, and in a hundred ways shows that he is interested—service to others, church attendance, and so forth.

How can you love Her? First, you must meet Her. Of course, the man who never prays can never learn to love Her. You must meet her through prayer.

Secondly, you must court Her. I realize this analogy is being pushed pretty far, and that many of you may be impatient with the erotic language of mysticism, but bear with me and it may suggest some thoughts to you. In courtship we use a great deal of flattery—not all of it is insincere. There is a great deal of honest praise, a constant pointing out of the other person's fine points.

Mysticism also has this element, for nearly all mystical prayers begin with very extravagant praise and thanksgiving. In fact, almost all prayer does. Almighty God, Most Blessed Lord, Heavenly Father, Merciful Creator, and so forth. The value of it is certainly not its effect upon Sophia, the Heavenly Wisdom. She is unmoved by vain flattery; but the effect on you is to stir up within you the feelings of thanksgiving, praise, and love. Many a man has stopped loving his wife because, after marriage, he stopped praising her; and many more men have never loved Sophia because they never praised Her, or thanked Her. We have much to be thankful for, the gift of Life itself, God's material blessings, which God showers upon us. Sophia's ever helpful hand is there whenever we desire it—all this without ever demanding anything in return. Surely all this should inspire love on our part, not that our love is purchased by God's generosity and gifts, but rather the gifts are evidence of God's love and we respond to it.

Lastly, you must be wedded to Sophia. You must be faithful to Her alone. You cannot love Sophia and materialism. You must choose between Her and all idols; the idols of lust, of wealth, power, fame and pride. You can be faithful to but one.

To do it, you must first be awakened, and know who you are, and what you are. You must know what you can be and what you must be if you are to have the love of Sophia.

You must purge yourself of all that is out of harmony with God's world, and stand aside even from yourself that you see only Sophia and nought else.

The path must be a disciplined one, consisting of good works, but above all, meditation. Through meditation, you seek the forgiveness of God, but most of all, you court Sophia's favor through words of praise and thanksgiving. You do not forget to give thanks and praise to Her for all that you have received and will receive throughout each and every day. You bring gifts, but most of all, you have fellowship together. It is not without reason that Boehme developed

106

prayers for every day of the week and for almost every conceivable act during the day. Perhaps the greatest practitioner of the art of prayer was Jeremy Taylor, who even had a special prayer for a man while taking a physic.

"Pray without ceasing" is the advice of the Scriptures, and for one seeking to become a mystic, there should be added two additional thoughts: "Make your life a prayer," and "Pray with a purpose."

The first is easily understood. Unless our attitude is one of love, words of love are vain and insincere. Unless we have given our hearts to Sophia, She will not treasure our words.

The second is summed up again in Scripture, "Do not pray vain repetitions." Any system of prayer that you can find will be for you "vain repetition" the first time you use it. It is not your prayer, for only by having the same experiences as the mystic who wrote it, can it ever be yours.

I would suggest that you work out your own devotional guide; one that expressed your thoughts, but more especially, your love for Sophia and then use it regularly. Until such time as you have charted your own course, you would do well to use the prayers of Jeremy Taylor, Jacob Boehme, Augustine, or just read daily from the great devotional classics, including the Bible.

Chapter XX

Union with God

"I became man for you. If you do not become God for me, you do me wrong."[1] These words of Meister Eckhart make the mystic's goal and expectations seem clear, and yet at the same time, they create confusion.

How can man become God? Before casting the idea aside as nonsense, let's think about the nature of man and about the nature of God. It does seem as if these two natures are mutually contradictory. How can man ever hope to become God?

But is this really a greater miracle than the fact that God became man? How can the mortal, imperfect and finite vessel that is man, possess the divine, immortal, perfect and infinite vessel that is God? Yet, God became man in Christ and did not Christ become Divine?

God is ever seeking to enter into the hearts and souls of men like you and I. He seeks us. Surely we cannot expect that should He enter our hearts we can ever be the same. Before He will enter into us, we must become a fit habitation for the Divine; but no sinner, no mortal and no imperfect man can ever hope to be a fit vessel for Him. For until we become like Him, that is, transmuted from man unto the divine essence, we shall not receive Him.

The deification does not mean that the personality is lost. Neither does it mean total and absolute identification with God. As God and Christ are one and yet different, so the mystic is one with God and yet different.

The Orthodox probably come close to defining the difference when they say that "The Son proceedeth from the Father." The Western Church has rejected this, since it implies that the Son is not equal with the Father.

But the mystic does not seek to be equal with God. It

---

[1] Evelyn Underhill, "Mysticism," The Noonday Press, New York, 1955, p. 420.

is in reality a spiritual marriage, and like marriage, the partners are one but not necessarily equal.

To seek oneness with God is not to seek to become as great, or as powerful, or as omnipotent, or as omnipresent. To seek oneness with God means, primarily, to submerge our wills in His. To love what God loves is to be united with Him in the best and greatest sense. When a couple becomes one, it is because they share all the things that matter.

To be united with God is to become a new creature, free from sin, from selfishness, from envy, from hatred, from possessiveness, in fact, all the things that separate us from God.

This state of being, or heaven, is truly a place different than anything we have known. The Pharisee had a very primitive notion of heaven, and although he could imagine it as a spiritual thing, he could not imagine it without the ordinary human institutions. He thought Heaven changed human forms, but he failed to recognize that it had need for none of the institutions and customs that we cherish so much. The words of Jesus, that in Heaven there is no marriage, must have seemed strange indeed. But marriage, as we know it, is not possible without possessiveness which is alien to the Kingdom of God.

Characteristic of the great mystics who have achieved this union with God are some attributes which seem almost super-human. They seem to have been lifted beyond the cares of this world.

So accustomed are we to thinking that the fear of death is a "normal" reaction, that we cannot imagine people without it. Once a person has been united with God, if only for a moment, all fear of death is removed. This is one of the best bits of evidence we have that a person has been united with God, for it is a certain sign that he has received the gift of eternal life.

The mystic tends to be unconscious of the fact that the fear of death has left him, for he has ceased to care whether he lives for the moment or forever. All he is certain of, is that he lives for God. This is sufficient. It is both a quality of the mystic and a sign that the mystic has truly been united with God.

Of what does this oneness consist? It cannot be a marriage of unlike substances, for such a thing would be a contradiction. Before the soul can unite with God, it must be purified in fire. All that is not Deity must be deified.

But, it is a marriage, and the two shall be as one. Like any marriage, the two shall maintain their separate identities. Husband and wife are equal, yet both do not give birth to young, and both do not possess equal power to hunt or lift heavy objects.

God alone has power and God alone is the Creator and Sustainer of Life! The mystic is not God, he is wedded to God, and he is one with Him.

There is no contradiction here, but there is mystery. To dwell in close intimacy with God is Heaven enough. The soul united with God is free from sin, and the desire for sin. Having perfect peace and fulfillment, it seeks after nothing that its Love does not also love.

In heaven, Jesus said, "There is no marriage." There cannot be, for the soul is wedded to God and seeks to possess and be possessed by God. This God he will gladly share with others and welcome them as Brides of Christ.

Only God is jealous, and only God shall possess each soul completely and fully. This completeness is exclusive. No man can possess another in the manner in which God possesses the soul who surrenders himself to his Creator.

In this union there is purpose and plan. All things are to be brought into relationship with the Cosmos.

The love that brought us to God will increase through us and bring others to Him.

This state is not one of unbroken bliss. For as we strive to bring others to God, we learn of disappointment, frustration, and of man's infidelity. We see mirrored in each man our own long history of rebelliousness. We relive our own failures and our own misdeeds; and though it ceases to matter, we suffer with all mankind. We, too, have our moments of "weeping for Jerusalem."

Yet, this service to God is our new life, and brings joy beyond our present understanding. The mystic has undergone a true transmutation. He no longer fears death, and the joy and peace which surround him are always a mystery to those whom he meets.

The seeming contradictions with sensual reality no longer bother him; nor is he disturbed by his inability to explain the source of his euphoria and his strength.

No man can be the same, having seen God. If he cannot explain what has happened to him, it is of small moment, for who can explain any of the great spiritual experiences that one enjoys throughout life.

Poets have balked at setting down in words man's love for a woman, and if this eludes them, surely man's love for God is even less capable of being expressed through word, painting, or any other medium known to man.

He has been to a world not seen by many. He recalls only dimly much of what he has seen. Even that which is clear cannot be told, for the man who has stayed close to home cannot understand and appreciate experiences so completely foreign to him.

We question the mystic so often on this point, and many doubts spring from our inability to understand. Yet, it is precisely on this point that we ought to be reassured. The experience and the Deity that can be grasped by a finite, sinful, and human mind must indeed be small and of no consequence. If the mystic had seen less than God, he could with ease tell us about his experience. But having seen, he is beggared for words, and he can only tell us to come and see for ourselves.

In the case of every mystic, their friends and even their enemies were not impressed by what the mystics said they experienced, but by the transformation wrought in them by their experiences. The mystics have not given us great words of theological wisdom, but from time to time, men have seen in them the presence of God.

When a man unites with God, it is no secret, for his transfiguration is seen by witnesses and hidden only from the most spiritually dead. The fact of a Union with God rests upon a great cloud of witnesses down through the ages who have seen men and women who have become ONE with Him.

Some scoffed, none understood, but all knew they stood in a Presence. Every awakened man seeks to be touched by this Presence, and for this end, purges his soul and longingly searches for the Divine Illumination. This is no chimera, but to the mystical mind, it is the reality before which all else melts into a foolish and vain illusion.

For some, union means fulfillment; for others, it is the ultimate and only reality; and this too, is a mark of the soul united with God, a certainty so sure, so great, that it must either be the mark of madness or the mark of the Divine.

Chapter XXI
How to Begin the Contemplative Life

You have already begun your search that marks your beginning as a contemplative. God has given man a curiosity about the world in which he lives and a hunger for the world he has not yet seen.

Whether you are reading this book out of curiosity or out of your hunger does not matter. For whether your interest springs from a desire to know, or a desire to fulfill the yearning of the soul, it does not matter now.

Read about those who have gone this way before you. But do not only read books about them, read their words. Tempt yourself with the descriptions of what they have found, what they have done, and what they have become. After you have stimulated your appetite through their experiences, you will truly be ready to begin your own journey.

If you are truly awakened, and not just wishing that you might be, you will already have considered your sinful state and how far you are from the Kingdom of God. Consider those things you have done whereof you are ashamed and seek the forgiveness of God. Try to understand the weaknesses within you that brought you to this state, and pray for God's strength and health that you may overcome temptation again.

Augustine, Boehme, and many others felt it necessary to write autobiographies which they called their "Confessions." It is a useful exercise if one is to understand fully the condition of his own soul. The great mystics knew much about God because, first of all, they took the trouble to learn much about themselves. Once a man fully comprehends the depths to which he has fallen, he must flee to God as his one hope and refuge. All men tend to think too highly of themselves, to gloss over their sins, and to inflate their good deeds. An honest appraisal will show each man the folly of trusting in himself and in the first few moments of honest appraisal, many have despaired.

Out of this despair, or dark night of the soul, one must step with faith. Do not ask God to save you from sin, for most of us cannot live but one day at a time. Ask God to help you live through *this* day without sin.

Prepare for yourself a systematic plan of devotions. No man succeeds in business unless he organizes his business life with extreme care and attends to it faithfully.

Columbus, when he set out to discover a new passage to India, prepared himself, his ships and his crew. Only when everything was in readiness did he set out and sail to the West.

You, too, are setting out on a journey that will take you far beyond any earthly journey, and you will not succeed unless you devote all that you have to its success.

Learn all you can about the mystics and their devotional life. Begin every day with prayer and plan the times during the day that you will lift your heart heavenward. No man is big enough to keep his heart and mind fixed upon spiritual things without some plan to keep himself from being swallowed up by the busy world about him.

Jeremy Taylor suggested that a man choose some natural reminder such as the striking of the clock, to take a few seconds to pray, that is, to speak to God.

During the purgation process, a man must pray often or he will surely lose heart. He must pray often or he will fall to temptation. He must pray often or he will not know right from wrong. Do not assume falsely that you always know when you are doing right. The mind is subtle and tricky; and we rationalize all too easily. No, if a man would do right, he will keep his soul sensitive to good by living constantly in the presence of God.

Do not seek signs from the heavens. In God's own time you will be illumined, and while you may enjoy its ecstacy, you will also be frightened by the experience. Growth is a painful process, and if the mystical life promises great joy, it also promises great sorrow.

Jesus, who promised others the abundant life, was known as the Man of Sorrows. John Epes experienced the "Dark Night of the Soul," and, in time, you shall experience it also.

You will be tested and tried, and if you have sought God for the right reasons, you will not be found wanting.

You cannot seek Him, as so many do today, in order to obtain for yourself the gifts of peace of mind, health, or even success. There are so many who seek not God, but only what they can get their hands on. No, you must seek Him for Himself alone. When you desire Him, and not what He can give you, your journey has begun.

If you find yourself believing that you ought to want God but have no hunger for Him, do not despair. There are other honest reasons for seeking Him, besides a great hunger. Some men seek Him because without Him they feel life has no meaning. The world seems irrational, and without order and they know that once they find God, the world will make sense, and they will find a rational place within it.

Others seek God, because they know that it was for this that they were created. Unless we seek Him, our time, three score years and ten, would be wasted. Without God, there is no purpose to Creation, and it would seem folly to let life pass without using life as God intended.

Finally, many are aware of God's great love for us. He gave us life, and then in love and trust, He gave us freedom to use it as we choose. We can even work against Him, as we do so often, and He does not destroy us. Nay, He continues to sustain us day by day and showers abundant blessings upon us. We may deny Him, hate Him, despise Him, and yet we live!

Our time is so short, yet we let days, weeks, months, and years go by without seriously seeking Him. Some, no most, let life go by without ever having seriously sought the Giver of Life. In all this, God is ever faithful, ever loving, ever ready to receive us.

This love cannot go without inspiring in many a desire to return this love. Even as He gives to us, so we wish to give to Him. We do it by our devotion, by the small gifts of our time, our talent, and our energies.

In our giving, our love increases and becomes much easier. After some time, if our devotional life is constant, our loving comes without His seeking it, and comes alive in us, and ultimately transforms us.

115

The mystical life is easy. It has no plan, but the plan you make. It has no form, but the form you give it. The one thing needful is that you seek God with all your heart, and all your mind, and all your soul. You cannot wish and hope to make it so, but this must become the one obsession, the one central purpose of your life. If you seek Him in this manner, you will discover that He was never far from you.

Bibliography

Anonymous, *The Cloud of Unknowing*, Harper & Brothers, New York, 1948.

An Unknown Mystic, *Prayers of the Mystic Way*, St. Willibrord's Press, Billerica, 1967.

Baker, F. Augustine, *Holy Wisdom*, Harper & Brothers, New York, undated.

Berlin, Isaiah, *The Age of Enlightenment*, Mentor Books, New York, 1958.

Blakney, Raymond (translator), *Works of Meister Eckhart*, Harper & Brothers, New York, 1941.

Buber, Martin (translated by Olga Marx), *Tales of the Hasidim*, Schocken Books, New York, 1961.

Bucke, Richard M., *Cosmic Consciousness*, E. P. Dutton & Co., New York, 1946.

Butler, Cuthbert, *Western Mysticism*, Constable Publishers, London, 1951.

Cheney, Sheldon, *Men Who Have Walked With God*, Alfred A. Knopf, New York, 1945.

Fenelon, Guyon & Molinos, *A Guide to True Peace*, Pendle Hill, Harper & Brothers, New York, undated.

Ferm, Vergilius, *An Encyclopedia of Religion*, The Philosophical Library, New York, 1945.

Gibran, Kahlil, *The Prophet*, Alfred A. Knopf, New York, 1923.

Gibran, Kahlil, *The Garden of the Prophet*, Alfred A. Knopf, New York, 1933.

Gibran, Kahlil, *Jesus the Son of Man*, Alfred A. Knopf, New York, 1928.

Gibran, Kahlil, *The Madman*, Alfred A. Knopf, New York, 1918.

Graef, Hilda, *Mystics of Our Times*, Hanover House, Garden City, 1962.

Hamann, Johann G., *Werke*, 5 Volumes, Thomas-Morus-Presse, Im Verlag Herder, Wien, 1949.

Harshorne & Reese, *Philosophers Speak of God*, The University of Chicago Press, Chicago, 1953.

Huxley, Aldous, *The Perennial Philosophy*, Harper & Brothers, New York, 1945.

Kelpius, Johannes, *A Method of Prayer*, Harper & Brothers, New York, 1951.

Kepler, Thomas, *Theologia Germanica*, The World Publishing Co., New York, 1952.

Merton, Thomas, *Seeds of Contemplation*, Dell Publishing Co., New York, 1944.

Mueller, Ernst, *History of Jewish Mysticism*, Phaidon Press, Oxford, 1946.

Nadler, Josef, *Johann George Hamann*, Otto Muller, Salzburg, 1949.

Nicholson, Reynold A., *Studies in Islamic Mysticism*, University Press, Cambridge, 1921.

Otto, Rudolf, *Mysticism East and West*, Meridian Books, New York, 1964.

Palmer W. Scott, Editor, *The Confessions of Jacob Boehme*, Harper & Brothers, New York, 1954.

Pinard, William J., *Mind*, Forum Publishing Co., Boston, 1959.

Pruter, Hugo R., *The Path of Love*, The Brownist Press, Berwyn, 1952.

Pruter, Hugo R., *The Theology of Congregationalism*, The Brownist Press, Berwyn, 1957.

Pusey, Edward, Translator, *Confessions of Saint Augustine*, Pocket Library, New York, 1958.

Shoemaker, Samuel M., *How to Become a Christian*, Harper & Brothers, New York, 1953.

Scott & Gilmore, *Selections from the World's Devotional Classics*, 10 Volumes, Funk & Wagnalls Co., New York, 1916.

Stace, Walter T., *The Teachings of the Mystics*, New York, The New American Library, 1960.

Smith, Ronald G., *J. G. Hamann*, Harper & Brothers, New York, 1945.

Steere, Douglas, *Time to Spare*, New York, Harper & Brothers, 1949.

Steere Douglas, *On Beginning Within*, New York, Harper & Brothers, 1943.

Stoudt, J. J., *The Way to Christ*, Jacob Boehme, Harper & Brothers, New York, 1947.

Sugrue, Thomas, Translator, *The Story of Edgar Cayce*, New York, Dell Publishing Co., 1958.

Sweet, William W., *The Story of Religion in America*, Harper & Brothers, New York, 1950.

Walker, Williston, *A History of the Christian Church*, Charles Scribner's Sons, New York, 1945.

Whicher, George F., *The Transcendentalist Revolt Against Materialism*, D. C. Heath & Co., Boston, 1949.

Young, Barbara, *This Man from Lebanon*, Alfred A. Knopf, New York, 1945.

www.ingramcontent.com/pod-product-compliance
Lightning Source LLC
Chambersburg PA
CBHW030519100426
42813CB00001B/90